LIZZA

LIZZA

Wendy Robertson

Hodder & Stoughton
LONDON SYDNEY AUCKLAND TORONTO

For Barbara, my mother

British Library Cataloguing in Publication Data

Robertson, Wendy
  Lizza.
  I. Title
823'.914 [J]   PZ7

ISBN 0-340-39119-7

Published by Hodder and Stoughton Children's Books,
a division of Hodder and Stoughton Ltd,
Mill Road, Dunton Green, Sevenoaks, Kent TN13 2YJ

Photoset by Rowland Phototypesetting Ltd,
Bury St Edmunds, Suffolk

Printed in Great Britain by Butler and Tanner Ltd,
Frome, Somerset

Contents

I Lizza at home

The brown hat lay like a nestling animal in the cardboard box. Mrs Donahue's claw-like hands hesitated a little before she lifted it reverently and passed it over to Mrs Bremmer.

'Married in it, I was. My mother sold her own mother's wedding ring to buy it. Good, I felt, I'm tellen yer.' Her voice was soft with Irish edges. She lifted the edge of her apron and started to rub her hands with it, applying hard pressure as though to punish herself.

'Well, I cannot see why you brought it round.' Mrs Bremmer stroked the hat, taking uncharacteristic pleasure in the mouse-like surface. 'You might have a special occasion, sometime.'

'Special occasion? Bless yer, Mrs Bremmer, when will I get another special occasion? Don't we both know that my days for special occasions are past?'

Mrs Bremmer stayed silent. Mrs Donahue had had six children in the eight years since her wedding and looked fifteen years older than her twenty-five years. The next special occasion she would enjoy would likely be her own funeral.

Elizabeth sat quietly on her perch on the fender, stretching her back at the fire's heat, and watching the two women. Her mother, her white oval face smooth and full, her black hair scraped back, was a tall plump pigeon while Mrs Donahue was a bedraggled sparrow nursing grey feathers.

'Now look, Mrs Bremmer. You can be sure I want Lizza to have the hat. The train she's travelling on, she'll have to wear a hat, a decent hat. She'll need a decent hat on a train. Only decent, it is.' Mrs Bremmer shrugged, still unwilling. Mrs Donahue became urgent, her hands still now, loosely hanging at her side. 'I really want to do yer a favour. Barney being laid off, you've done so much for us. How many times is it that Lizza would come round with pasties or broth or bread new baked?'

Lizza's mother, unwilling as always to accept anything, stared dubiously down at the hat. Mrs Donahue turned round to Lizza, looking down at her as she sat on the fender. 'Here, lovely, try it on!' She took it from Mrs Bremmer's hand and very carefully, tucking Elizabeth's loose red curls behind her ears, she placed the hat on her head and pulled it tightly down at a flattering angle. 'Beautiful pet, really lovely! Goes lovely against that white skin. And it just catches them brown eyes.'

Elizabeth stood up, turned on tiptoe and looked into the glittering wood-framed mirror above the mantelshelf. She, Elizabeth, looked in; a strange woman looked out. Fourteen years, but really twenty-four years. She felt disappointed, uneasy. Disgustedly, she pulled off the hat and shook out her hair so that the impress of the hat vanished, making it fall in its usual thick mass.

'Careful now, lass.' Her mother's steady tone was slightly reproving. 'Don't be rough. It's a very good hat and it suits you.' She turned to Mrs Donahue, smiling gently. 'We thank you, Mrs Donahue. A very nice hat it is for Lizza to go to Bradford in.' Somehow it seemed as though she were doing Mrs Donahue an enormous favour. She stood there, her face stern, full but finely drawn, her black hair pulled severely back. She glared at Elizabeth who dared make no objection.

The hat was carefully nested again and Mrs Donahue stood up, wiping her hands down her long faded apron in preparation for departure. She hesitated. Elizabeth's mother waited quietly. She never gossiped. Mrs Donahue would have loved to sit down for another ten minutes. Mrs Bremmer knew that any little query would have given her a loophole, would have allowed her to linger a while. She was determined that it should not happen. She picked up a yellow stoneware piedish lying on the iron shelf above the coal fire.

'Here. That'll be something to get into you and the little 'uns.'

Mrs Donahue murmured weak protests even as she eagerly took the fragrant burden. 'Thank you, Mrs Bremmer. Be sure I'll get the dish back to you tonight.'

Mrs Bremmer smiled regally and nodded as Mrs Donahue scuttled away, her boots stamping on the scrubbed stone flags. Lizza sat down on a high-backed bench that stood up against the side wall. She sat quiet, lost again in the sinking feeling that had invaded her ever since her mother had told her of tomorrow's journey. She pondered again the terrible fact of being sent away, as she rubbed with her forefinger at the highly polished wood on the bench beside her, making a greasy spot against the satiny sheen.

Her mother moved efficiently round the kitchen, laying the table, setting plates and dishes to warm on the iron fireplace, stirring the pan of potatoes that was bubbling on the flames. Elizabeth watched the coruscation round the blackened base of the pan, and turned her face sideways and closer to share the licking warmth, to feel the hot glow on her cheek.

Her mother noted the dead quietness of the child, her customary determined withdrawal. She turned the spoon round in the potatoes. How many times had this happened in fourteen years. She spoke: 'So, you're all set now. You've got the blue coat and the new shoes. The hat'll just make the difference. I'll parcel up your old boots –

they'll do just for work. And you can have one of my nighties. Our Ivy'll be pleased to see you. Really pleased, Lizza. She needs some company, that far away from home.'

Lizza looked up from where she was rubbing the wood really hard.

'I don't want to go, Ma.'

Mrs Bremmer felt the familiar helplessness in front of her fifth child's strength and determination. None of the others would have come right out with it. She hardened herself.

'No point in saying that. You got to go. There's no job here, girl, just service. An' you don't like that . . .'

No, she hadn't liked that. Skivvying resentfully for Mrs Martindale. Walking there for seven in the morning. Not getting back till eight at night. Even later, when people came to the festive dinners, when the Martindales entertained the other doctors and the vicar. She thought about the night she had walked back alone through the dark town over the last remaining bit of rough moor which separated the upper from the lower end of the town. She had thought she heard a baby cry in a clump of bushes. Taking a deep breath she had gone across, only to find a large black cat howling away.

In service she was both dissatisfied and unsatisfactory. She disliked being told all day long what to do and how to do it, and her superior air and her sharp knowing tongue had brought complaints of arrogance. In the end she had quoted Shakespeare at the housekeeper and been sacked for cheek. Mrs Bremmer tightened her mouth at the thought of the bustling, superior housekeeper who had come to the house to insist that her daughter was untrainable.

'If it's not service, it's nothing, round here. There's hardly any work for the men, with being laid off all over the place. And with no money around the shops won't take any more people on.'

'Why me though, and not our Beatrice or Renee?'

'Well you know, lass, Bea's got her job at the shoe-shop and Renee's fixed up in service at the Snowballs'. Anyway, Renee's done her stint away.'

Lizza rubbed harder into the wood, pursing her lips to stop the tears. It was true. Renee had been away. In service to Scarborough. She had been there a week when she returned home, in tears and homesick.

'But she was seventeen, Ma. Even she came back. Not so easy to come back from Bradford. That's much further.'

Mrs Bremmer was standing with her back to the licking fire. She was astounded at herself for even discussing the matter with the child. She was used to the law-laden nature of her own words. Even Bernard, who was twenty-two and working, did what she said without question.

'She was sick for home. Different, you are. You got more off now than she had when she was seventeen. A home-girl, she is.' She heard the note of approval in her own voice, and felt again the futility of talking to the child. She glanced at the ticking clock, tall and grandfatherly, in the corner. She lifted the potato pan off the fire and took it into the back kitchen; leaning back to counter-balance the weight of water and potatoes, she began to pour off the boiling water. She shouted back into the kitchen, her voice abstracted by the task in hand, masked by the steam.

'Yes. Different you are. Always were. You'll cope better. You'll manage better on your own.' Her tone, even through the half-open door, was accusing.

Lizza leaned against the carved back of the settle, thinking bitterly about the difference. It was there. She had always known about the difference. There were times when she had enjoyed it.

As she mashed and creamed the potatoes, Alice Bremmer thought about the difference. As far as she could tell,
it had begun with a severe attack of rheumatic fever the
child had suffered at the age of eight. She had nearly died.
Afterwards she had been ill for so long that her mother
was forced to relax her rules of hard, clean, pious living,
instant obedience and domestic order. Lizza discovered in
those months that she could fight and win a battle of wills
with her mother. The rheumatic fever had been followed
by a prolonged physical disturbance, a kind of twitching.
Lizza used this in what her mother recognised as her final
battle. It happened one Sunday. Sundays were kept
religiously in that household. Chapel in the morning, in
the afternoon and at night; all cooking done the day
before; Bibles and religious books to be read, hymns to be
sung in the evening. One Sunday she came upon her
daughter sewing clothes for a doll.

'Now, girl. What do you think you're doing? Put that
away on a good Sunday!' Her voice had been sharp.

Lizza had looked up and very carefully bitten off a
thread with her teeth.

'Well, Ma. Don't you remember the doctor saying it
was absolutely imperative that I kept my fingers busy, all
the time?'

Her mother had been stunned. She was hot with rage
both at the impudence of the statement and the superior-
ity of the vocabulary expressing it. However, there was no
denying the literal truth of her statement. Not one of her
other children would ever talk to her like that. Except Ivy,
of course, and she was already gone. Then there was the
reading. Although all Elizabeth's three sisters and her
elder brother had been good scholars and read well, they
didn't bother to read books. In the evenings and at
weekends, they made things, played games and walked
out with friends. Lizza read. Anything and everything, in

any corner and in any space. She had one favourite place. There was always a clamour in the warm kitchen which left no space in her brain to hold and savour the stories she read. However, in the corner of the kitchen was a mangle that was always covered with a clean and pressed white table-cloth. Underneath was a private space. She liked it in there, reading in the filtered white light, shut away from the voices and the domestic clatter.

Her mother had found her there one day when the room was empty, and had uncharacteristically lost her temper, shouting about the uselessness of books and demanding why she could not help in the hard work of the house rather than wasting her time with them.

Alice Bremmer forked the top of the potato into an elaborate criss-cross pattern. She liked her food to look good. Ivy had been a queer one, too. Uncontrollable almost from the first, more like a boy than a girl, but not as biddable as a boy. It wasn't books with her. It was fights. She was always fighting with boys as well as girls, always avenging slights on herself and her friends. In the last three months before she had gone, six different people had knocked on the door to complain of her violence and wickedness. In the end her mother had taken a strap to her and she had run away to Bradford. How she got there was still a mystery.

Within a week a letter had arrived, in a flourishing hand:

Dear Ma, Bernard, John and girls,
    Well, I arrived here after a long journey. I went straight to a mill and got signed on and they sent me to the lodgings. You would not believe the size of this town and its big buildings and the people with money here. The shops are really big and full of lots of things. When I get my first pay I'll buy you something, Ma. I miss

you all and wouldn't mind a bit of your meat and potato pie, Ma. The food here doesn't touch yours. There is lots of work here. All the women round here work. It would be nice if one of the girls could come, now I know the place.

Love,
Ivy

She had read the letter many times, the first one since the letters she had had from Jo when he was in France. Those letters that had come with regular insistence right through the war and had ceased abruptly, finally, six weeks before armistice. He had written letters which gave her, right through the war, a spark of his energy, a shred of his humour. It didn't seem like eight years since she'd had one of those letters.

As she took the potatoes into the kitchen, Lizza was rubbing her eyes and looking up defiantly, her lips pressed together in a hard line. That hard defiant look robbed her face of all the grace it normally enjoyed, with its sensational combination of white skin and fiery chestnut hair.

Alice went across to the fireplace, picked up a large golden-crusted pie, and put it on the table beside the dish of smoothly-mashed potatoes.

'Seeing as you're here, you can have your dinner with our Bernard.' Even as she spoke, the gate clicked and the boots came clumping down the yard. There was a pause as he sat to take off his boots, a rustle as he hung up his work jacket in the back lobby, and a rattle as he dumped his bait-tin and helmet on the table in the scullery. Then there was a splash of water as he washed his hands and face in the kitchen basin. Alice listened to these ritual sounds that had been part of her life as long as she could remember. Her father, her brothers, her husband, then after the four years gap of the war, her son.

'Hello, Ma! Now, Lizza!' He nodded at them both, his face still grimy but his eyes smiling from one to the other. 'Dinner ready? My, I am hungry!' He sat down heavily on his chair, and Lizza pulled hers up. 'You having yours too? Last dinner at home with your big brother?' He started to laugh but stopped when he saw Lizza's grim face and his mother's urgent shake of the head.

They bowed their heads in a few seconds' conventional prayer before they started, then ate in silence, while their mother looked on, standing silently at the fireplace. Bernard only spoke when he had finished eating.

'Nice that, Ma,' and sat back peacefully in his chair.

'Good shift, son?'

'Heavy. Eighteen inches. Plenty water. Rumours that another twenty men're being finished. There's a lot of feeling about. I don't know. They say they want us to increase the hours. No more pay. Something'll happen.' His young, blackened face pursed itself in concern and he was silent for a moment. Then he looked across at Lizza sitting silently in front of her emptied plate.

'What about you, young 'un? You all ready for your big journey?' He purposely ignored his mother's frown.

'Yes, I'm ready. Mrs Donahue gave me a hat to wear for the train. I don't want to go, though.'

'Lizza, we'll have none of that.'

'Leave her, Ma. It's only natural she doesn't want to go away from home. It's a big step – but not such a bad one, Lizza. You're going to a job, which is like gold these days. And you're going to our Ivy. Just like one of those stories you read. You'll like it, believe me.'

Lizza felt some comfort. Bernard always gave her a sense of calm, a feeling of order and organisation in life. He, like her, was clever and always seen as different. He left school early because he knew all they could teach him. He had found a good job in a shop, which he liked. In the week he was to be fifteen he had come in from the shop and joked with his mother.

'Well, Ma. What can I have for me birthday?'

'The pit! You can have the pit.'

It had been a grimly uncharacteristic joke but the next day he had gone to the pit and signed on. He had done well, getting his deputy's certificates at nineteen, and throwing himself into the life. He loved the pit, he had a growing understanding of the geology of that region, an intelligent instinct for the logic of the art of mining. He liked nothing better than to talk to the men who had worked underground for twenty years, about the stone world under the ground with its moods and movement.

He would be sorry to see his sister leave. He liked her company. She listened to his tales of coal, and told him of the stories she read, and read him bits of Shakespeare from the collected edition given to her by one of her teachers.

He had been troubled to note the growing tension between his mother and Lizza since the girl had left school. The pair were too strong for one hearth. His mother liked to be in total unquestioned control. She allowed him some power and direction because he was the man of the house, and brought in a wage. Even so, the condition of obedience to the powerful woman ruled his life.

He wondered if she had always been that way. He could remember the brief leaves his father had had from France. The first time, before the army had set up delousing facilities, he had been lousy. Bernard thought now of the laughter in the yard as his father leaned against the kitchen door, dressed only in clean, pressed, pit shorts. The stench of ammonia filled the air as his mother used tongs to hold the filthy uniform over the tin bath, and the lice dropped with tiny splashes into the boiling water.

They had laughed so much that she had finally sent him into the house so she could concentrate on the important job in hand.

Lizza, too, could remember that first leave. She must have been about three years old. Da had got her mother to dress her in her best dress so that he could walk her up to the town in his newly-cleaned uniform.

He had taken her hand and, looking up, she could see the shiny brass buttons and the red cropped hair. They seemed to walk for many miles, and her legs got so tired that he put her, with easy strength, up on one shoulder.

Finally they arrived again at the bottom end of their street. At the corner was a cluster of men, some squatting, some standing. They were hovering and waiting till the pub opened. He put her down.

'Now, pet. If I watch you do you think you could walk all the way back to see your mammy?'

She had felt uncertain.

He had laughed then, and taking her over to the little front-room shop that was tucked in beside the big pub, he bought her a bag of green apples from the fat, shawled woman behind the counter. He gave the bag to her, and she had had to use both hands to carry it.

'There now, me little flower. Take that home and give your sisters and Bernard one each.'

She was satisfied, and as she made her way up the long street she kept looking back so she could see him squatting there, waiting, looking smaller and smaller. When she thought of him now she always thought of him like that, squatting and waving, the afternoon sun making a torch of his red hair and glittering on his uniform buttons.

The three of them were silent, her mother like a statue at the hearth, Bernard leaning his face on his hand, pushing his cheek up awkwardly. Lizza was inside herself thinking of her father, somehow having caught the thought from Bernard.

Bernard spoke. 'I've got a union meeting tonight at Ben Compton's. Six o'clock. We've got to talk about what to do about this new thing about hours.'

'No need to make trouble, Bernard, you've got a job and you need to keep it.'

'Important, Ma. Some families only have the man's wage to depend on. Not as lucky as us . . .' His voice faded.

'Lucky?' His mother's voice was bitter, but there was an ironic truth in what he said. There might be seven of them but their family at least had the security of a tiny war pension which was always there and did not depend on the whims of employers and governments.

Lizza was impatient, unheeding of the interchange, and stood up to go.

'Hey, hold on, young 'un.' Bernard stopped her. 'I've got something for you.' He jumped up and went upstairs, leaping downstairs a minute later. He gave her a little parcel of brown paper, tied with cotton.

It was a brooch. A gold bar with a gold claw-set pearl in the centre. She ran a finger over it then pinned it to the neck of her blouse, looking again in the mirror over the mantelpiece.

'It's lovely, Bernie. Where'd you get it?'

'Feller at work was selling it for his sister, whose man's out of work. Hester Jones. You know. Like it, Lizza?'

'Yes. Barbary pearl and gold.'

'What's that?'

'Milton. *Paradise Lost*.' Bernie smiled at her.

They looked at each other and their mother bustled to clear the table.

'No use sitting around talking rubbish. Better get your bath, Bernard, before our Johnnie gets in from school.'

She lifted the lid of the boiler beside the fire and allowed a pleasing gush of steam to rise.

'You can go and meet'm from school, Lizza. Get the milk from Newmans' while you're out.' It was a command, not a request. Alice wanted the house clear while Bernard had his bath.

Lizza hovered at the door, thanked Bernard again, and went off quickly at her mother's sour glance. The houses backed on to a lumpy stretch of green which was scattered with huts and hutches housing hens and rabbits and sometimes even a pig. The pigs had always been good to watch, growing from small, pink, wriggling things into massive tub-like animals, still with the same wise, tiny eyes buried in fatty wrinkles. Sometimes the children lit fires on the green, to roast potatoes or turnips taken from the fields, or to bake fancy buttons and animals from clay you could dig from a certain part of the green. She liked doing these, but always alone.

There were already children coming down the back from school, among them Clara and Maggie Donahue. Clara, the older girl, had a dark face and brown skin with heavy brows and upper lip which made her look angry even when she wasn't. Little Maggie had the same heavy upper lip, but had full-open eyes heavily shadowed underneath. They both wore dark dresses covered with dirty print pinnies, and boots. Maggie's pinny had a big hole in the front, showing the dark dress underneath.

''Lo, Lizza,' Clara shouted across the width of the lane. 'Your Johnnie got wrong again. Got the stick for not knowing his nine times.'

'He knows his nine times.'

'Well, he wouldn't say them.'

Lizza shrugged and walked on, passing more and more children dressed like Clara and Maggie, some cleaner, some just as dark and dirty-looking. Lizza looked with satisfaction at her own skirt and blouse, handed down and made over two or three times. But at the last make-over her sister Bea had embroidered flowers down the front of the blouse, and both it and her skirt were clean and pressed. She ran the edge of her thumb over Hester Jones' brooch.

'Now, Lizza!'

Johnnie's jumper was skewed up over his flannel shirt, his cap was across to one side. He grinned at her. She nodded.

'Clara Donahue says you got the stick.'

''S'right. Old Nobbles came in and told us to say me nine times. An' I didn't.'

'Why not? You know your nine times.'

''Cos-for.' The usual final chanted answer. No point in pursuing it.

'Anyway, we got to get the milk at Newmans'.' She indicated the metal-lidded milk can in her hand.

'I'm not.'

'Ma says we got to.'

'Me and Sam's going playing buzzers.'

'You'll get wrong.' Playing buzzers involved stuffing drain-pipes with paper and rags and lighting them. The consequent fire made a huge buzzing sound if properly set up, and caused panic in many households.

'Won't get caught. Go on, Lizza. You can get the milk yourself. I'll meet you at the gate and we can go in together.'

'That's lying by implication.'

'What's that mean?'

'It means, yes, go and create a bit of panic and I'll see you at the gate in twenty minutes.'

He gave her a thump on the arm that jarred her, then raced off, his rusty short-cropped hair glinting in the pale February sun.

Newmans' farm was just at the end of the long street, set like a wedge into the town, with the farmyard at the point. Lizza made her way down the yard, picking her way between pools of sludge and inquisitive chickens. She knocked on the heavy green-painted kitchen door and waited for a whole minute before it was opened by Mrs Newman, a full-faced woman in a coarse bleached sack apron.

'Hello, Mrs Newman. Can I have a pint of skimmed milk?' She proffered her tin-can. Mrs Newman nodded pleasantly enough, and, taking the can, went across the yard to the dairy, and brought back the can brimming over with the frothy skimmed milk.

'There you are, Lizza. That'll be three-ha'pence.' She pocketed the coins. 'You not at work today?'

'No. I left. Didn't suit me.'

'Job not easy to come by though, especially now.'

'I'm going away to work. Near our Ivy. In Bradford.'

'Oh, that'll be nice. I hear there's more jobs going down there – and more money. Your ma'll miss you, though.'

Lizza smiled and nodded, but didn't say anything. She put the lid on the can.

'Thanks, Mrs Newman. I'm going away tomorrow, so I won't see you for a while.'

'Well, you'll be a miss, Lizza, I'm sure I wish you luck in your new job.' Then Mrs Newman did a very strange thing. She formally shook Lizza's free hand. Lizza was embarrassed. No one had ever shaken her hand in that way. She turned away awkwardly, said 'I've got to go now,' and ran, oblivious of the slimy puddles, through the farmyard and out of the gate.

Once on the long back lane she stopped running, slowing her walk almost to a stop, swinging the milk can in her hand. The lane was very quiet. She could see some children playing on the other side of the green, and there was a woman in a black shawl walking away a good way ahead of her.

She started to swing the can harder, forward and back in a releasing rhythm. She was taken with a desire to swing the can right over her head. She had seen other children do it, but she was forbidden to do it, it was frivolous and silly and a dangerous thing to do. She swung it higher and higher at the front and the back. Then, the final delight, right up and over. A good feeling. A complete circle. Try it again. And again.

The third time round the lid came off when the can was at its highest point, clattering to the ground as the milk sloshed down on her, soaking her hair, her blouse and all down one side of her dark skirt. With sinking heart she started to run. Being seen like this in the street was only marginally worse that the scolding she would get from her mother.

'She'll murder you.' Johnnie's voice, as he met her at the gate, was gleeful. She pushed him violently out of the way and raced into the kitchen. Bernard was sitting reading, scrubbed clean and handsome in white collarless shirt and black trousers. Her mother was busy with the table again, laying it for Johnnie's tea. They both looked at the same time, and she thought with one part of her mind how alike they were, pale and dark and full strong faces.

'Lizza!'

Bernard was amused, her mother furious, at the playfulness and the waste.

'Good thing you're going away, girl. Maybe you'll learn to grow up. Maybe you won't have time to get into mischief.'

'Mother!' Bernard warned.

Lizza slammed upstairs, stripped off, and set about cleaning up the damage. By the time she had washed her hair and her blouse, and sponged down her skirt and herself, her mother was busy again laying the table for the girls, who usually got back together at half past six. Renee, who worked as a housemaid at the top end of the town, usually called for Bea as she finished her work at the shoe-shop.

They were laughing as they came in, arm-in-arm, from the stark evening into the lamp and firelit kitchen. Lizza, sitting at her usual place on the wooden settle, looked at them fondly, desperate that she wouldn't be here the next night to see their cheery homecoming.

She was equally fond of both her older sisters. They were so different, although they were dark and pale-faced. Bea, the eldest, was beautiful. Large dark eyes, smooth skin, pale small hands. She was quiet and reserved, a sense of humour more passive than active. She never told or made jokes, but she laughed very appreciatively at other people's. In the house she had always been her mother's right-hand woman, almost matching now her mother's skills at the cooking, cleaning and sewing that was the sacred ritual of her life.

Renee was the joker. Broader and squarer than any of her sisters, she was a person who always saw the funny side. She told jokes and played jokes on people. Even at seventeen she liked to go out and play ball games with the younger children. Lizza was very close to Bea, going to her rather than to her mother if she needed comfort or help.

The two girls sat down to eat their meal and their mother poured tea for all the other members of the family, who sat round the table to talk and exchange the stories of the day.

The story of the spilt milk was told with relish by Johnnie, accompanied by disapproving asides from his mother. Bea smiled, but Renee laughed out loud.

'That's our Lizza, always dreaming. I wondered why you were sitting in your shift and topcoat.'

'Did you get the milk out?' Bea was domestically concerned, as always.

Lizza nodded.

'Well, I'll have a look for you to make up any damage. Oh! I brought you something. Look in my basket.'

Lizza jumped up and went to Bea's basket. There was another brown paper parcel. In it was a collection of ribbons, a comb and a brush.

'Mr Drummond got them for me to give you. I told him you were off tomorrow, and he said to make sure you took care of your hair. A "unique feature", he called it. He said not to let them persuade you to get it cut.'

'Thank you, Bea.'

'Me too,' Renee spoke with her mouth full of piecrust. Mother was out in the scullery. 'Look in my basket. Under my apron.'

It was a mirror in a tooled leather frame. One corner was faintly clouded, but the leather was highly polished.

'They put it to throw out' – Renee always called her employers 'They' – 'with a pile of letters.' Bea always read the discarded letters. 'Some good ones there. Show you them at bedtime.' Bea shushed warningly as their mother returned to the kitchen.

The rest of the evening was spent in the quiet routine of washing-up, and cleaning boots and shoes. Then at nine o'clock they carried a lamp into the faintly cold sitting-room, with its harmonium in the corner. Renee sometimes played, but normally their mother played softly, music-ally, while they all sang; Bernard in a clear baritone which directly reflected his mother's Welsh background. They always sang hymns, this was all she would play. She finally closed the book, indicating that she would stop, but they protested, asking her for one more.

Very softly she started to play and one by one they joined in the familiar song:

> '*There is a green hill far away*
> *Without a city wall,*
> *Where the dear Lord was crucified,*
> *Who died to save us all.*'

Lizza, standing behind her mother, felt the tears falling. She let them fall, not seeking her handkerchief, so that no one would notice. Renee's arm went round her shoulders, and from the other side, Bea's arm went round her waist. All three of them kept their eyes on the music and sang on.

2 *Journey to Bradford*

'You'll be all right, Lizza, really you will.' Renee's square, strained face made a lie of her statement. She clutched her young sister's forearm. Cruelly, Lizza looked away through the waiting-room window, refusing to meet her sister's gaze, rejecting even the counterfeit of comfort. The station was veiled in rain which dripped down the gutterings on the station buildings and gathered in puddles on the platform.

The waiting-room fire flared away, welcome heat in the late winter chill. They stood to one side of the fire, Lizza's parcel and small suitcase on a polished chair beside them.

Another family were clustered in the waiting-room – a tall man in a soft dark coat and leather gloves standing staring out of the window; a woman sitting at the other side of the fireplace with three children clustered about her. A girl and two boys. The girl wore a neat maroon coat with a fur trim on the collar. The delicate, finely cut lines of the coat made her look dainty, unused.

Her pale eyes had little colour in them. They wandered round the cosy waiting-room and settled on Lizza. She stared at the hat; her pale strange eyes worked all the way down to Lizza's shoes, then back to the hat again.

Lizza pushed her hands down into the pockets of her thick blue cloth coat, and scowled at the slight reflection of the hat that showed itself in the window, her face an unseen shadow underneath.

The girl detached herself from her mother's side and walked across to Lizza. She put her hand out and stroked the rough blue fabric of the coat, smiling not at Lizza but at the firm weave of the blue material. Lizza left her own misery for a moment, thinking the action reminded her of Emily Sargent. Emily had been in the same class at school. She, too, never looked at people, only things. She too had a way with her.

'Iris!' The man's voice was strong but not severe. The woman rustled up. 'Iris, dear. Don't bother people.'

'She's all right, missis. Really she is.' Lizza found herself with her hand on top of Iris's small one, pressing it closer to her arm.

'Well,' the woman's voice was doubtful. 'She doesn't seem to understand, you know.' Her voice trailed away. Iris had turned her head to hold on to Lizza. 'Well, if you don't mind.' She turned back to sit down and the man continued to stare out of the window. Still holding on to the girl, Lizza turned to pay more attention to the family. The two boys were younger than the girl, both around ten, she thought. They might be twins although they did not look alike. The dark one was clutching a green metal train and the fair one was turning over the pages of a book. They whispered together. Lizza found herself straining to hear what they said, but it proved impossible.

Outside the waiting-room, in the covered area of the platform, were three working men with heavy jackets and big boots. The tell-tale parcels under their arms indicated that they too were going away from home. One was quite young, no older than Bernard, but whiter-faced and much thinner.

The door opened, letting cold and damp flow into the hot waiting-room. Her mother came in. She looked a stranger with her thick outdoor coat on, and a close hat pulled down over her hair. She looked at the girl clinging on to her daughter, then came across to speak to Lizza in a tone unusually gentle for her.

'There you are. Keep this ticket safe.' She was tucking it

inside the home-knit wool glove on Lizza's free hand. She pulled back the welt and slipped in the ticket, as though Lizza were four, not fourteen. She tucked a silver half-crown into the pocket of her blue coat. 'Our Bernard sent that for you, as well as the ticket money.' She paused. 'Well, what do you say? Have you nothing to say?' There was a sharper thread in her voice, more like her usual tone.

Renee reached out and squeezed Lizza's arm.

'Thank you, Ma.' She finally turned to Renee. 'Thank you, Renee, for coming to see me away.'

Renee had slipped away from her place for an hour to see Lizza off. She had bartered the hour between eight and nine for the promise of two hours on Saturday afternoon, when she was usually free. The housekeeper had been pleased with the bargain.

''S'all right, Lizza. I wanted to see you on to the train . . .'

The other family were getting up, the mother smoothing her fine coat, the boys pushing their books and toys into their pockets. The girl finally released Lizza's hand and went to stand quietly by her mother.

Mrs Bremmer looked the small, fine-faced woman in the eye.

'Could I ask you if you are going to Durham?'

The woman looked timidly at the man standing at the window.

'Yes, we are.' It was a whisper; conspiratorial.

'My daughter needs to change there to get the train to Bradford. I wonder if you could just look to her. See that she gets on the right train. You see, she's never been on the train before.'

'Yes. Yes, I'm sure I can do that. We ourselves are going to Bradford, so we will see that she gets the right train.'

'That will be quite convenient.' The man now spoke from behind them. They all turned guiltily, as though discovered in a felony. 'How old is she, and what is she called?'

'Her name is Elizabeth. And she is fourteen.'

Lizza was furious at being talked about as though she were a thing. The man looked down at her over a large brown moustache, catching the furious glint in her eye. He did not smile but the corners of his eyes creased, a ripple of humour.

'Well, our name is Bamburgh. This is our daughter Iris and our sons Fergus and Johnson. They are thirteen and ten years, respectively. Our daughter Iris seems to have taken a fancy to Elizabeth.'

Respectively. Lizza had never heard the word used out loud before. She savoured its use and, in that, lost her anger.

The rattle and hum of the line foretold the coming of the train, and they gathered up their parcels and packages. By the time it was gushing steam and soot they were standing at the edge of the platform to feel it swirling round them. And the smell. For always afterwards Lizza would associate the oily, sooty, steaming smell with this particular parting. It would always particularly compound desolation and adventure, the safe familiar and the threatening unseen.

Mr Bamburgh put all the bags on the wooden racks, including Lizza's small case and parcel. She kept the cloth shoulder-sack that Bea had made for her, with her name embroidered on the flap. In it were the comb, the ribbons and the mirror, a plate pie for her dinner, a new handkerchief, and her collected Shakespeare. Bernard had said that everybody read on trains and to take a book to read.

Mrs Bamburgh put her beside the window, and Mr

Bamburgh sat opposite her. Looking down through the
open window she suddenly thought how fragile her solid,
capable mother looked in these strange surroundings, her
hands together, almost as though she were praying. Her
face was white as always, and showing no emotion. Renee
beside her was standing like a sack of potatoes, arms
loosely by her sides, silent tears tumbling down her face.

Lizza stood up and leaned out of the window and smiled
broadly, her facing aching with the effort.

'Don't worry, Renee, I'll be all right. Really I will.'
Renee, not recognising the echo of her own words, sent up
a watery smile. The girl Iris wriggled in beside her. 'I'll
write to you, Ma, and tell you how everything is.' Her
mother nodded slowly. Looking down on them, she felt
older than both of them, and as the wheels started to turn
and the steam wreathed round their dark pale-faced
figures, her heart lifted. She couldn't think why.

The country outside flashed past, rising green hills
marked here and there with the tell-tale cones of slag
heaps and the not-too-distant wheel. She was dizzy with
the speed of the train and trembled at the constant
movement. It was new. She had been on a motor-bike
quite a few times, and that was strange enough. But here
the swaying, rattling movement, the noise and the speed,
made her feel dizzy. She closed her eyes.

'Are you all right, dear?'

She opened her eyes. The flower-faced woman was
talking to her, a timid concern in her face.

'Yes thank you. It's just funny. I haven't ever been on a
train before.'

'Well, you'd better get used to it. After Durham you'll
have a few hours to get used to it.' The woman's voice was
soft, accented like Lizza's own but with more definition –
all the words were given their full dignity, the endings
particularly clear.

Lizza fiddled in her cloth bag and brought out the thick, stubby edition of Shakespeare.

'That's right, dear. You read. It'll take your mind off it.'

The children watched her stonily as she fiddled to close her cloth bag, and place it on her knee with the book on top of it. She opened it at her marker and started to read.

'Heavy going for a girl. What are you reading?' The man looked across at her. His voice was heavy and more distinctly local than his wife.

'*Henry V.*'

'I wouldn't 'a thought you could read that.' His face settled back on its chins and the sides of his mouth came down in cruel lines.

She looked scornfully into his gritty eyes. 'I know it off by heart.'

The larger, darker, boy called Fergus spoke:

'I don't believe that. You couldn't.' There was a faint sneer in his voice. The man smirked. 'A big claim, that. Can you back it up by telling us some of o't?'

She looked around at the others. The flower-faced woman was smiling and nodding. The girl, unsmiling, looked out of the window as though she heard nothing, but still she leaned heavily on Lizza. The boys raised their brows and exchanged a look of insulting disbelief.

She took a breath:

> '*This day is called the feast of Crispian.*
> *He that outlives this day, and comes safe home,*
> *Will stand a tip-toe when this day is named . . .*'

She forgot the people, loving the words as they rolled on and linked together, thinking how Bernard had loved her to say it for him, in the late evening firelight.

'Very good, dear.' The woman's voice broke her dream.

She looked up, round at the faces of the family. Iris's face was now vacantly on hers, a slight smile on her lips. The boys' faces shared some respect. The parents exchanged a glance.

Johnson, the fairer, slighter boy, spoke.

'Good that. Was it in a war? I like that bit about showing the fears. Do you know any more?'

'Now Johnson, don't press Elizabeth too hard.' Mr Bamburgh looked at his watch. 'We'll be getting into Durham in a minute. We must gather ourselves together.' He reached up for the cases.

The train lurched and slowed, ran straighter and smoother, then finally stopped with its windows wreathed in steam.

Elizabeth climbed down with her bags and parcel and found her mouth filled with the sooty steam and her ears filled with the clatter of movement of the station.

'Now then, young woman, follow us. The train is on the other platform.' Without waiting for an answer the big man strode off, and Elizabeth found herself scuttling along behind him with Iris, ahead of Mrs Bamburgh and the dawdling twins.

At that same time on Durham station, Roland King, who one day would know Lizza, stood huddled into his heavy school overcoat, clutching his school cap somewhere in the region of his stomach. He looked at the two men standing beside him on the platform, talking across him as though he did not exist. Mr Glanton, his teacher, like a fat owl, with a broad face that gave a deceptive appearance of benevolence. He was known at school to show no mercy, and King knew no mercy would be shown to him when he finally arrived back at school. Mr Silkin was small, slightly bald and sandy with dusty lawyers' black clothes.

'I can only say, Mr Silkin, that we at the school are at the end of our tether with King's defiance. He refuses to meet the school's very reasonable demands for a certain level of behaviour, a certain standard . . .'

'I understand, Mr Glanton, I understand. And I am grateful on behalf of Commander King that you have shown leniency towards the boy. If he didn't go back to school I don't know where he would go, with his father at the other side of the world.'

'Well, I must repeat, Mr Silkin, that we at the school are at the end of our tether, the very end. One more transgression . . .'

'I'm sure, quite sure, that it will never happen again.' Silkin finally peered full-face at King, his face stern. 'We'll have no more running off. Stay and stick it out, take your father's example. Be a man.'

King avoided the lawyer's glance and his eye went along the platform to the collection of people waiting for the train south. The men continued to mumble on over his head. His eye stopped at a family group. Three younger children and an older, slightly plump sister with penny bright hair swept up under a dark hat. No, not a sister. A maid perhaps. Very pale face and dark eyes. He caught her eye and she pulled an aggressive face at his obvious cheek in staring. He blushed and turned his face to Mr Silkin who was now thrusting his hand into his.

'Now Roland, sharp honour. Stick it out and respect your elders. I'm afraid I must write to your father about this.' He bustled away leaving behind a stale miasma of sweat and old books.

'Now, boy, come!' commanded Mr Glanton, and strode along the platform and down the hill, at a fast pace for a fat man. All King could do was scurry after him, resenting the smirk of the red-haired maid who had seen the whole interchange.

There were two men sitting in the only carriage which still had space. An older man with a thin face who could have been any age between thirty and fifty, and a younger man – a boy – with a shock of black curly hair and startling jewel-bright blue eyes. They were both pale with the familiar shadowed cheeks of people living perpetually on this edge of hunger. There were paper parcels up on the string-net rack, and the men wore heavy-duty boots that had seen better days.

They shuffled along to make more room, and the younger man stood up to put Lizza's parcel on top of his on the rack. He smiled slightly and nodded to acknowledge her thanks.

The large man and his wife were sitting opposite them with the twins beside them, so Lizza had to sit beside the men, with Iris nestling beside her. She wondered if it had been manoeuvred this way so that the dust from the men's clothes would be insulated by her blue flannel. She put her embroidered bag on her knee and leaned back against the seat, closing her eyes. She tried to conjure up the faces of Renee or Bea, or anyone from home. There were lights and colours and shooting stars under her lids, but not a familiar face anywhere. She gritted her teeth against the itching in her nose that usually preceded the shameful tears, those forbidden signs of human weakness not permitted in her life at home.

The train lurched. There was a clattering slam of doors, loud authoritative shouts. The train shook and shuddered again, and there was a swinging grind and an efflux of steam as the train started.

She kept her eyes closed and let the rhythm take her. It was quite pleasant really, being shaken, rattled and swung from side to side at the same time. A flowing ripple seemed to be rushing up her body from her toes to her head. Suddenly the flowing ripple caught in its path the

ingested contents of her stomach. She clamped her mouth
shut and stood up in a panic looking at the world racing
past the window. No way out!

'Here.' The young man had hold of her arm and was
dragging her to the door. She thought desperately that he
was going to throw her off the swiftly moving train. In the
event, he fiddled with the leather strap and dropped the
window. Then he grasped her shoulders and thrust her
head out of the window. She was mercifully and completely sick. The rushing air forced itself over her face and
into her mouth, making her feel fresher and much lighter.

The boy pulled her back and sat her in her seat. His
hands were thin but strong, like steel pincers. She put her
hand to her head. Mrs Donahue's hat was gone. She
panicked, then relaxed. Good thing. She hadn't liked it
anyway. She smoothed the front of her hair and adjusted a
pin in the back knot.

'Are you better now, dear?' Mrs Bamburgh's watery
face looked anxiously across at her.

'Yes. Much better now.' She smiled reassuringly as
though she was the older person. She turned to the young
man.

'Thank you.'

He nodded and half coughed but didn't say anything.
His bright blue eyes passed from her across to the window.

'Do you know any more about that poem, about that
fight?' The fairer twin looked across at her.

'Fergus. The young lady is ill.' Mr Bamburgh spoke.

'No, really, I'm all right now.' She looked into the eager
eyes of the twins. Their sister sat passively picking the
edge of Lizza's sleeve. Her mother leaned over and took
her hand away but it immediately returned.

'Well, I don't know if I can go through the whole of
Henry V but I do know this other poem, about how Horatio
held the bridge.'

'Can you say it, then?'

So, the next hour was taken up with Elizabeth and the boys saying the poems they knew. In the end even Mrs Bamburgh joined in with a poem about a cuckoo:

> '*Oh blithe new-comer! I have heard,*
> *I hear thee and rejoice . . .*'

Mr Bamburgh looked on kindly and the two men in the corner watched with guarded interest, the older one nodding and smiling now and then, showing dark-gapped teeth.

The recitations faded and everyone sat back in their seats and watched the scenery. Towns flew past. They stopped at many stations, entertained briefly by the people getting off and the people getting on; the prancing self-importance of guards and railway officials. Mr Bamburgh pointed out York Minster to Lizza, massive but lighter-coloured than Durham Cathedral. Not so good, thought Lizza, not having its own attendant castle.

Mrs Bamburgh started to fiddle with one of the baskets, moving a cloth to reveal a nest of other cloths containing bulky items. She opened these to show sandwiches and cakes. Lying along the bottom was a bottle of lemonade, its top sealed by a white pottery stopper wired on tight.

The boys shouted with delight and eagerly took the sandwiches offered. She put one into Iris's hand and closed the girl's fingers round it. Mr Bamburgh refused. She offered one to Lizza.

'No, thank you. I have my own dinner here.' She fiddled with the embroidered bag to get at the plate pie.

Mrs Bamburgh offered a sandwich to the silent men. The young man reached forward. The older man coughed and leaned on him so that he couldn't reach. 'That's all right, thanks, we got our own.' He put his hand into one of his deep coat pockets and pulled out a newspaper parcel, and out of the other he brought a corked bottle of water. The young man did the same. They opened their parcels to reveal potatoes, baked in their jackets and allowed to go cold.

Fergus whooped. 'Baked potatoes!'

'Fergus!'

'Don't bother, missis. He can have one if he fancies.' The man picked out the biggest from his pile and palmed it across to Fergus.

'No.' Mr Bamburgh's voice was firm. 'You mustn't take it, Fergus, unless you exchange yours for his.'

Fergus looked down at his sandwich with meat lapping over the edge. Grinning, he held it out. 'That seems fair.'

After that, there was an orgy of swapping so that everyone, except Mr Bamburgh, had a baked potato and everyone, except Mr Bamburgh, a sandwich and everyone, including Mr Bamburgh, had a piece of Lizza's plate pie.

The train seemed to be going faster now. The clicks were merging into a hum and the world was whirling streaks of green and grey in the sectioned frame of the train window.

Mr Bamburgh brushed back his moustache with the two middle fingers of his right hand, brushing away the last crumbs of pie.

'Your mother, Elizabeth, must be a fine cook.'

'Well, it was our Bea that made the pie. But she's not so good as me mother. So you're right.'

Mr Bamburgh raised his eyebrows slightly, smiled, and showed pale yellow teeth. He turned to the men.

'You'll be going south for work, n'doubt.'

'That's right.' The older man nodded. 'Nowt up here. I was laid off four years ago after the big strike and no work since. The son's just been laid off. No work to get. A lot of bad feeling about as well. Say they're trying to drop wages.'

'In the pit were you?'

'Yes, all me life, save for the war.'

'What kind of work will you get down in Bradford, then?'

'Dunno. Anything. Mills. Transport. Anything. I can drive. I drove in the war. Tanks . . . but it's six and two threes, driving. All th' same.'

'How about you?' He turned to the younger man.

'Dunno. I got me deputy's tickets, but I don't know whether it counts for anything down there, skilled men. Mebbe send money home. Mebbe settle.'

There was a heavy silence as the train raced on. Lizza and the twin boys mirrored the seriousness in the adults' faces. Johnson, the darker twin, spoke up, relieving the tension.

'You were in the war, mister?'

'Aye, son.' He nodded, half smiling.

'What was it like? D'you get any medals?'

'It was muddy and cold. Not like that Horatio at the bridge. But there were some brave men there too. I did get some medals, but there was plenty even braver got none. Plenty of me mates died, doing what they had to do.'

'You drove tanks?'

'Yeah. Just before the end of the war. They were drier than the trenches.' He looked at Mr Bamburgh. 'Did you get out there, mister?'

The larger man cleared his throat. 'Unfortunately, no.'

'Nowt unfortunate about that . . . a lot of good men died. No need for it.'

The looks of eager interest in the twins' faces was fast fading. Mr Bamburgh took out a notebook and wrote something in it, then tearing a page out, handed it to the older man.

'That's the address of my work place. We make some of the small parts for the machines in the mills. There might be some kind of work for you. Don't know about the lad, but he might get fixed up . . .'

The father and son exchanged pleased smiles, but their thanks were cut short by the lurching and grinding of the train as it drew to a halt, and the flurry of clothes and bags and people as they prepared to alight.

Before Lizza knew where she was or what was happening she was on the platform. The two men, whose names she still did not know, had vanished, and there was a milling crowd around her. The noise was deafening. The high vaulted roof of the station echoed the shouts and calls of the people and the hiss and clatter of the trains. She had never in her life heard so much noise at once. She put one woolly-gloved hand to her ear to cut out half the sound.

'My father says you must come.' Fergus spoke to her and led the way to where the family were standing among the lumps and rectangles of their baggage.

'Ah, Elizabeth.' Mr Bamburgh looked down at her. 'Do you know where you're about to go?'

'My sister is to meet me. My mother wrote to her.'

'Well, doubtless she'll be here soon. Anyway, here is our address in Bradford.' He handed her another sheet of paper, like that he had given to the men.

'Yes,' offered Mrs Bamburgh, 'please call to see us after you settle in Bradford. Perhaps you will come and say some more poems for us?' Her voice sounded faint, but quite eager. 'Iris has taken to you. And the boys.' She was quietly disengaging Iris, for the fifth time, from Lizza's coat.

'Yes,' chimed in Fergus. 'Some more fighting stories.'

She hesitated. She didn't really want to take it. She wasn't like the men with nowhere to go, and no money. But they were looking at her so expectantly. Even Iris, who had hardly spoken to her at all, was smiling, very faintly, though not looking directly at her. She really was like Emily Sargent, who'd been at school with her from the age of five.

She took the paper and stuffed it into the embroidered bag.

'I thank you. It is kind.'

Mr Bamburgh was thrusting bags and boxes into the children's hands and heaving up the large case himself.

'Well. You watch yourself. Bradford's a big place after Brack Hill, I know, meself. Came here when I was not much bigger than you. Take care.' He nodded and set off purposefully through the crowd. His family, all except Iris, smiling at her each in turn, scurried after him. They reminded her of the ducks she had seen so many times at Newmans' farm.

Her heart became solid again and she sat down to wait for Ivy. She thought she would have liked to say goodbye to the men. She was still sitting in the same place two hours later when Ivy actually came. It was only three months since Lizza had seen Ivy but she didn't recognise her. She had short-cut hair, only just skimming her collar, and her mouth was painted an unlikely red.

3 *Staying with Ivy*

Ivy Grant, née Bremmer, raced on to the platform at six o'clock to see her young sister sitting on the end of a barrow, her feet dangling awry, reading a book. She breathed a sigh of relief. Having to meet her young sister had warped her day. In the first place she had had to tell Gilbert she wouldn't be able to go to his friends' pub. He had been annoyed because he had promised that Ivy would go and give a hand. In the end, with his usual combination of sulks and threats he had persuaded her to go 'just for an hour.'

Then, as usual, in the middle of the singing and the fun she had been unwilling to come away. She had ignored the niggle underneath the top level of her mind. At last the clock in the pub sitting-room had struck six, and she had jumped up dramatically and raced for the tram. Now she walked up to the crouching figure, who looked up at her approach. Unseeing. Unrecognising.

'Don't you know me? It's Ivy.'

The pale face smiled, rather hesitantly. 'You look different.'

Ivy tossed her bobbed hair and pursed her red lips.

'Everything's different here. You'll find out. Come on, then. Let's go.' The child made her uneasy. The still, white face made her think of her mother, and she was resentful at being dragged away from the life and fun of the pub, so she gave no apology or explanation for her lateness, and Lizza knew better than to expect one.

The creaking and the swaying of the tram was another new experience. It wasn't quite like the train. It was colder. There were perpetual draughts from the door, making Lizza huddle down further into her blue wool coat. The tram emptied and filled itself at every stop. There were so many people, getting on and off the tram, so many people on the pavements, and if you peered very hard, inside the shops. There could hardly be so many people in the world. How could a person see so many people and not know one?

She did know one, of course. Ivy was sitting beside her. Her thick black hair had been cut short, flat across the eyebrows, with fat forward curls over the ears. Looking down, Lizza could see the long, graceful legs which ended under the seat in front in black shoes with heels like cotton bobbins.

Sitting now beside Lizza on the tram she smelled of violets, a foreign and strange thing. She was not the wild tomboy who had vanished from the house six months before.

'What do you think of it then, a'kid?' Her voice and words were funny too. Rougher in all sorts of ways, more like the quacking voice of other people on the tram.

'It's big. A lot bigger than Brack Hill.' It was a criticism but Ivy didn't pick it up as such.

'Yes. Plenty happening here. You did the right thing, coming.' Her black eyes snapped down at her young sister. 'I got a job fixed up for you in bobbin shed at place where I work. Had a word with foreman.' She didn't say any of her *the*, making a kind of noise with her nose to indicate where the *the* should have been.

'That's good. What kind of job? What would I have to do?'

'Dunno. Thirty shillings a week, though. An' it'll be easy enough.'

Thirty shillings! Bea's wages would only come to that in

three weeks. All these people, all these buildings and thirty shillings a week.

The tram swayed to a stop, easing and settling on to its wheels which were locked into the metal runners. Ivy swung into the aisle behind Lizza, grabbing the steadying leather strap as the tram jerked, and Lizza could see her narrow shape under her soft coat. As it jerked the man waiting behind Ivy lurched into her and there was some joking and banter that Lizza couldn't hear.

Lizza jumped off first, dropping her paper parcel as she did so. She bent down to pick it up and some pins came out of her hair. She bent down to pick them up, and came up with a red face to see both Ivy and the man, young with a greasy face and a large moustache, laughing at her.

'Here. Give us them.' Ivy took the pins from her hands, and pinned her hair back up, tucking a stray red strand behind her ear. She turned to the laughing man at her side. 'She looks old enough but she's no age, really, to be away from her mammy.'

Lizza, smelling the sickly violets again, tugged her head away from her sister's grasp, and started to stalk down a street of narrow high houses, her heavy shoes ringing on the cobbles. She turned in response to the second shout from behind her. Ivy, a smaller figure now, was yelling 'No good, Lizza, wrong way.' She pointed upwards to a road which had the same high houses, the same cobbles. 'This is where we go. Come on. Don't take the huff. You get away, you.' She gave the man quite a friendly push. 'Me sister's scared to death o'you and I ar'n't surprised.'

He smiled and shrugged and walked off, back in the direction from which the tram had come. Lizza slowly walked back to Ivy. She was in a rage that was hard to keep down. She felt like spitting at her sister, and the anger stopped the sad and hopeless feeling that had engulfed her since she sat on the station.

As she reached Ivy, her older sister took her parcel from her, and her little case, and put her arm through hers. Lizza could smell the violet scent again. She kept her elbow rigid, rejecting the soft hand.

'Oh come on, Lizza. We got to live together now, so it's no point in starting bad friends.' Lizza let her arm go soft, which allowed Ivy to squeeze it, express some affection. They started up the hill together.

'Things are bad up home, then?'

'There's no work. Plenty of people out of work, even them in work don't get much money. Bernard says they might even knock down the pitmen's wages.'

'Yeah. Better down here. Plenty of work up to present. The pitmen did themselves no good when they had that strike a couple of years back. All you do is lose the work you got, Gilbert says . . .'

'Gilbert?'

'Aw heck. I was coming to Gilbert. The thing is, I'm married now.'

'Married? Ma . . .'

'Doesn't know yet. Didn't really want to tell her in a letter. Better face to face. And I haven't been back since to tell her face to face, that is.'

The hill was steeper here, and they were both struggling, so they saved their breath for their effort. At the top Lizza spoke.

'What's he like?'

'Gilbert? Oh, you'll soon see. Here we are.'

It was a tall green door in a tall house. There was coloured glass in the shape of a hedge-rose above the door. Lizza liked that.

Inside they were in a narrow hall with a staircase leading upwards. Ivy led the way up. Lizza enjoyed the new feeling of carpet under her feet on the stairs. The stairs at home were scrubbed nearly white and clean, and your feet quietly thudded away. There were grease marks on the edges of the carpet and rolls of fluff here and there.

In the middle of the third flight was a small landing with a door off it. Ivy led the way through the door to a large room, done like a sitting-room with what seemed like hundreds of ornaments, and a roaring fire in the grate. In the corner was a large double bed covered by a crocheted spread, done by Ivy herself, Lizza was sure. There was one on Lizza's own bed at home, its very twin, that Ivy had crocheted before she went away. All her sisters had 'good hands' on them – like their mother, they could make anything.

'So this is the one who all trouble's been over?' The voice was behind her. She swung round to see a man standing in the doorway with a kettle in his hand.

Gilbert was a tall, fair man with a red face. His features were roughly modelled but soft, like the faces Lizza used to make with left-over dough from the baking.

'Quite the beauty then, Ive. Well, Lizza, ain't you got a kiss for your new brother?'

Before she knew where she was, he had put the kettle down and was clasping her and kissing her on both cheeks and finally on her mouth. She stood still, her hands clasped together in front of her, pushing slightly against him.

'Leave off, Gilbert. Lizza's tired from her journey. She 'ad to wait at station 'cos of you.' He stepped back and grinned at Lizza, showing two brown teeth at the front.

'Don't you believe her, Liz. Your sister don't do anything 'cos of anyone else 'cept herself.' He picked up the kettle again and put it on the hob. 'And here am I makin' yer a cup o' tea. What d'ya say to that?'

'Thank you.'

Ivy was grinning from one to the other. 'Here, Gil. You mek tea and I'll show her where she's to sleep.'

Ivy led the way out to the landing and up the next narrow flight of stairs. There was only one door on the tiny landing, narrow, more like a cupboard door. It opened on to a small square space, with a bed with iron rails and brass knobs. There was a small washstand, a cupboard, a rail of ornate copper hooks mounted on a wooden board, and a tiny window.

'No cupboard for ya clothes, Lizza. But it's nice and clean. Cost yer five shillings a week.'

'Five shillings?' Lizza's eyes were wide.

'I know, I know, you can rent a house for that up home. But yer not up home now and anyway, y'd only get five shillings a week for skivvying for somebody from dawn till dusk. Out o' thirty bob you can afford five shillings, and anyway places are hard to get down here, y're right close to centre here, you know.'

Lizza put her embroidered bag on the bed, took off her coat, laying it beside the bag.

'Well. D'yer like it? I went to enough trouble to get it. Mr Mac – that's the landlord – took some persuading and only agreed if Gilbert and me fixed this place up. It was just a place where they kept the boxes before.'

'It's nice, Ive, really it is.' She looked round. The ceiling came down at one end, and the carpet was frayed, but it was neat and clean. 'I really like it, Ive. I an't never had a room on me own. I'll like that.'

'Will you?' Ivy was dubious. 'I never liked that part of it meself. Up home there was always somebody to kick or to cuddle. Sometimes think that's why I grabbed on to Gilbert so fast.'

'I like to be on me own.'

''S'all right, honey. Y'll have to be on your own here, with me and Gilbert working. And then there's helping out in the Gantry on a night.'

'The Gantry?'

'Well, it's a public house. Don't you go telling Ma when you write. It's just me and Gilbert go there to help and sometimes to meet our friends. But don't tell Ma . . .' She resented the anxiety in her own voice. 'And don't tell her about Gil. I'll do that when I go up next.'

Lizza sat on the bed. Tell Ma! You'd just as well tell her that Ivy supped with the devil each night. She'd be no more shocked. She crossed fingers on both hands, not knowing why.

'No, Ivy. I won't say anything. Really I won't. And I like this little room. It's like a little rabbit hutch.'

There was a man's bellow from below.

'There's Gilbert. The tea'll be mashed now. And we got some shop cakes for you coming. Come on.'

4 *First day at work*

Lizza was playing on the green. She was carefully putting clay into a tin lid, then, with a stick, making the round shape into a face with round eyes and hair flat across the brows with curls each side. Then she carefully heaped up sticks and scraps of coal and set fire to it with a single match rescued from her apron pocket. She watched as the fire flickered and darted then settled in a hard red glow. The clay would fire up nicely, she thought. The head would make a good one for her collection.

Right across at the other side of the green, a long way away she could see the tiny figure of her mother, waving wildly to her with both hands, shouting, 'Lizza, Lizza!'

She tried to get up, but couldn't. Her legs wouldn't move. She struggled frantically but her legs were welded to the grass, as though they too were clay like the head under the flames.

'Mammy, Mammy! I'm coming.' With one final heave she managed to get to her feet, and stand upright . . .

She was sitting upright in a strange bed. A small room like a cell with a window high in the wall.

'Lizza, Lizza!' The door rattled and, recognising Ivy's voice, she remembered where she was. She swung her legs out of bed, padded barefoot in the dim morning light to the door, and turned the key that was lodged in the lock.

Ivy was standing there in a blue dressing-gown with dragons embroidered on the lapels. Her hair was immaculate and her lips were in place. She had a little oil lamp in her hand which supplemented the dim early-morning light.

'You must'a been dead to world.'

'Yes. I was dreaming. I thought you were Ma, calling me across the green.'

'No time for dreaming, lass. Gotta get to work. Show willing, you know, show willing. Here.' On the floor beside her she had placed a steaming jug and a small bowl. 'Get yourself washed and come down to ours for some breakfast. Only bread and tea, mind, but it does.' She padded away in slippers with feathers on the top.

Lizza swilled her face and put on her clothes from yesterday. She looked at the heavy boots her mother had parcelled up for her and threw them as far under the bed as she could. She pulled on the lighter shoes, still dusty from the train.

The three of them walked in the company of hundreds of others in the dawn twilight. The swirling crowd of people walked in one direction with very little talk, the human noise made up of the hard clack of boots and shoes and the boom of clogs. People called greetings to each other . . . 'Aye, Jack,' 'Now, Freddie!' but there was little conversation. Lizza ran a little every five steps to catch up with Ivy and Gilbert, who had a fast customary rhythm and were talking across her head as though she wasn't there. They came to a large flat wall, with a door as big as a house let into one side.

'There, see. That's Sydney's. That's where we go.' Ivy clutched Lizza's arm and pointed downwards.

Straight up from the pavement were windows like half moons, dusty, dark. Inside, swinging lights illuminated big weaving machines as yet untended, before the start of the shift. Shadowy figures moved about one by one, taking positions near the looms, removing hats and shawls, folding them carefully and putting them under the machine, in a safe place.

The door that was as big as a house was half open to let in the early morning flow of people.

'Gil goes on from here. Works for Terney's in the office. That's farther down the road here.'

'Yeah,' said Gilbert. 'See that black chimney on the left. The big one with the brick line halfway up?' He sprinted away, his boots striking sparks off the pavement, a workmanlike contrast to the faintly shiny serge suit that proclaimed office status.

Ivy led Lizza through the big door to a glassed-off office in the corner of the delivery bay. She knocked on the door and responded to the roar inside by pushing it open. The tiny office was all desk and chair. The desk was covered by papers neatly stacked, with three spikes empty, waiting for sacrificial victims. The man sitting at the desk was small and grey-haired, narrow faced like a whippet, with glasses on the end of his nose. His skin was brown, as though he had been in the sun for many months. She could smell old sweat and dust and warm wool.

Ivy lifted her arm and put her hand up on the doorpost. Lizza was aware again of the slim outline of her body.

'Now, Mr Singer. I got me sister here. Can you remember me telling you?'

'So I do, Ivy. So I do. Let's see.' Ivy pulled Lizza forward and squeezed her through the door.

He stood up and pushed his glasses up to the bridge of his nose. 'She looks young, Ivy.'

'I'm fourteen.'

'Have you worked before?'

'Yes. I have.'

'Where. In a factory?'

'No, a shop. Then in somebody's house.'

'Mills aren't like that. Hard places, mills. Don't think she would do, Ivy. Too fresh. They'd eat her for breakfast, that lot in there.'

'She'll be all right, Mr Singer. They're tough where we come from. 'Ti'n't all looks, you know.'

Lizza spoke up. 'I can do anything you ask. Anything. And I don't let people eat me up.'

He laughed. 'Same bottle, too.' He turned to Ivy.

'Tell you what, Ivy. I've a little job in the bobbin room, with the old'ns. They won't chew folks up much. Teeth's wore out with a lifetime on the shop floor.'

'Right then. I'll get off and get on, Mr Singer.' Ivy pulled down the little jacket with the frogged fasteners that she wore against the cold. 'Thanks for the favour.'

'No favour, Ivy. There's still a few jobs around for good workers.'

Ivy shrugged and drifted away and Lizza waited, awkwardly clutching her embroidered bag. He looked down, shifted some papers together and stood up. He was small, smaller than Lizza herself.

'Right. Come on then. Let's get you started.'

It was then that the noise invaded her. A clattering, clacking storm funnelled through from the tall door that led into the main factory. The little man touched her elbow and led her through. It was impossible to talk. The great machines pounded and clattered in savage unison. The women who tended them appeared to be having conversation despite the noise, their mouths and arms moving in communication. She trotted along beside the little man as he walked briskly through the mill, nodding and signing to people as he passed. He didn't smile. His mouth was turned down as he nodded the return of a silently-mouthed greeting.

The noise oppressed her. How could anyone work in it? Even scrubbing for Mrs Martindale had been better than this. At least there she could scrub away on her own and hear her own thoughts.

'Here!' Mr Singer tugged her arm and mouthed the word. They were at a heavy door set in a wall. It was closed and creaked as he pushed it open. He shut it with a bang behind them so that the clattering sound was muffled.

They were in a square room with three or four large tables. Old women were sitting round them, fiddling with what looked like oversized bobbins. The walls were made of lapped wood and the room was cold despite a little fire burning in a grate in one corner. The women wore heavy shawls; some wore two – one round their head and one over their shoulders. They looked at her without once stopping their fingers as they wound and finished the bobbins in front of them.

'I got some help for you girls. This is Lizza. Sister to Ivy Bremmer.' A fat old woman with glasses like marbles at the far end of the table started to cackle.

'Shut that, Joan. This'n's straight down from the country. I've brought her in here so she gets a proper gentling.'

'She'll get that in here, Mr Singer.' The woman who spoke was younger, with grey hair braided round her head. She had no scarf on her head and sat nearest the door. She smiled at Lizza, a brilliant warmth in a bony face. 'You'll be all right here, duck.' She looked again at Mr Singer. 'What d'ya want her to do? Shelve the bobbins?'

''S'right. I thought you could use some young legs in here.' A mutter of assent travelled round the tables.

'There you are, Lizza, your job'll be mainly to shelve the bobbins. But make yourself useful generally. See to the fire and keep the floor clear. This is Mrs Cobbett.' The woman with the braided hair stood up.

'You just leave her to me, Mr Singer.'

There was a shadow of a smile on Mr Singer's face, a

mere folding at the corner of one end of his mouth. Even this early in the relationship Lizza knew it to be a rare smile.

'There y're then, young 'un. Let's see how you get on. Mind, we only keep you if you work. No room for idlers here, no matter what Ivy's told you.'

She protested. 'Ivy never said . . .' but the heavy door was clanging shut and Mr Singer had vanished.

A soft hand was on her elbow. 'Come on then, I'll show you what to do.' The woman with braided hair – Mrs Cobbett – was steering her to a corner where there was a large basket, twice as big as an ordinary shopping basket. Mrs Cobbett hooked it over Lizza's arm. As they walked back to the large table Lizza noted that the woman walked in a very one-sided way. One of her feet dragged across the floor.

'Now, you take the bobbins that are finished and stack them in your basket, like this, see?'

As they collected the bobbins, Mrs Cobbett told her the names of the women who were working so swiftly, so deftly. They finally came to Joan, the toothless old woman at the very end.

'And here's Mrs Salter. Everybody calls her Joan. She's been workin' on the looms since she was eight. More than seventy years old now but still going strong. Her ma was a cottage weaver in the old days.'

'So she was,' the old woman cackled. 'Working at home 'stead of a great prison. So you're Ivy Bremmer's kin. Are you like her, then?'

Lizza changed the basket, now heavy with bobbins, to the other arm. 'I should think I probably am, since we're sisters. Though I don't really know, seeing she's been away from home for nearly two years now.'

'So, you think you probably are,' the withered voice mimicked. 'We can only hope you're not too like her in some things!' The women on either side of the old woman laughed.

'I don't know what you're talking about. And you can stop laughing,' Lizza planted the heavy basket on the ground and glared at the old woman, who was smiling knowingly at her, like Johnny sometimes did when he had the better of her.

'Now, Lizza. No cheek.' Mrs Cobbett reproved her. 'And you can just keep your ideas to yourself, Joan, or I'll have you out'a this shed and into workhouse sooner than summat!' The old woman's toothless grin faded and her face turned sour as she caught up another bobbin. 'Bring them through here!' Lizza picked up her basket and followed Mrs Cobbett's one-sided gait through an open doorway to a long room which had rows and rows of racks stacked with bobbins of all colours and shades. The racks reached high into the roof and there were ladders leaning up on them. The rising mist of colour rain-bowed the space. 'Your job is to stack the bobbins in the right place!' Mrs Cobbett helped her, and while they were doing this a door in the far wall opened and a dark, thickset young woman came in, carrying a basket like the one Lizza was using. She smiled and called a greeting to Mrs Cobbett and, referring to a scrap of paper in her hand, selected certain bobbins from the racks.

Lizza returned with Mrs Cobbett to the bobbin shed and was given the job of sweeping the floor until more bobbins were ready to go out. She spent the morning sweeping, sorting, carrying and clearing, and piling up the fire until her back ached and her hands felt dirty. As she worked the old women talked kindly enough to her, asking her how old she was, where she had come from, and telling her tales of the young ones in their own family.

After what seemed like ten hours of walking and lifting and carrying she was suddenly aware of a silence. The drumming of the machines had stopped. Like the ceasing of a heart in a great body; a death. One by one the old women completed their tasks, carefully tying off ends and stacking bobbins at the centre of the tables. Lizza put down her basket. Mrs Cobbett called across: 'Just take them few in, love, then you can stop for your dinner. No good leaving a job half done.' Wearily Lizza picked up the basket and took it through to dispose of the bobbins. When she came back the women had cleared spaces on the bench in front of them and were eating food from paper packages and scraps of cloth.

'Here, love,' called Mrs Cobbett. 'Come and sit by me and get your snap.' Lizza came across. 'Snap?' she said, uncertainly.

'Yes. Dinner. What do you call it when you bring your dinner to work?'

'Bait, we call it. But I didn't bring any.'

'Dear me. Your Ivy should've . . . Never mind, I got some spare.' She broke off half her sandwich and held it out.

''S'all right. I'm not hungry. Really not.'

Mrs Cobbett smiled faintly. 'Oh come on, lass. A growing girl like you can only be hungry after workin' as hard as you have. An' if I can't share my snap with you how can I ask you to do me a favour when time comes? An' come it will, you believe me!'

Reluctantly Lizza took the sandwich and ate it ravenously and was suddenly engulfed with kind offers from the other women around the table, of bits of bread and home-made biscuits. As she ate her way through these she felt the tears falling down her cheeks and into her mouth, making her sweet biscuits taste salty. Suddenly Mrs Cobbett's arm was round her and she was being rocked backward and forward, and the hard faces of the women showed only kindness.

'There, love, there. You'll soon get used.'

As the final siren went, Lizza was again caught with a full basket so she went to empty it on to the shelves before she could get ready to go. When she got back to the shed all the women except Mrs Cobbett were gone. The lame woman was standing with a shawl over her head and shoulders on top of a thick coat.

'There you are. I thought I'd wait for you. Thought mebbe you wouldn't find your way out.' She stood quietly while Lizza buttoned her blue coat. Lizza smiled up at her while her fingers fiddled with the belt.

'Thank you for waiting, Mrs Cobbett.'

'Don't think on't love. We all have to start sometime.'

'I think our Ivy'll be waiting for me.'

'Well, let's go and see.'

They walked as quickly as Mrs Cobbett's leg would let them, through the darkening mill with its silent looms creaking and settling for the night. The sweaty, rank smell of people was still about the place. However, when they reached the entrance place it was deserted except for the shadowy figure of Mr Singer in his glass cage. He saw them through the glass, came out and, shaking his hands in his pockets, leaned against the wall.

'Well, Mavis, how's she done?'

'Right good, Mr Singer. A proper little worker, this one.'

'Good. Good. Get off home then.'

'Have you seen our Ivy, Mr Singer?'

'Why, I think I did. One o' first out as usual. Went a good ten minutes ago.'

Lizza gritted her teeth, her face set in a grim mask.

'Find your way back to Ivy's place, can you?'

'Yes, I think so.' Lizza thought of the vast town with its maze of streets, like a huge wood with every tree a house.

'Don't worry, Mr Singer. I'll teck her. Just a step different from me.'

'Good lass, Mavis. These streets can be a loser for newcomers.'

Mrs Cobbett looked down at Lizza. 'Come on then lass. Best foot forward. Now that's an easy choice for me. Here, let me teck your arm. It'll be a treat for me to have a young arm to lean on, 'stead of stumblin' away on this gammy leg o' mine.'

Lizza offered her arm and slowly they made their way up the street, now dimly lit with high lamps. Mr Singer watched them till they vanished into the dusk shadows and returned to his glass cabin, shaking his head and muttering obscurely to himself.

Mrs Cobbett stood at the end of the street and watched as Lizza found the house with the coloured fanlight. She turned and waved and saw Mrs Cobbett hobble out of sight. She had no key, so she had to knock on the door. It was answered by a small man with round glasses and fair hair that was too long, contained behind rather large sticking-out ears. He smiled with crooked teeth and not much warmth in his eyes.

'Yes?'

'I'm staying here. I came yesterday.'

'Oh yes. Ivy's sister. She didn't tell me you were such a young 'un. Come on in.' The accent was strange yet familiar. Lizza remembered Ivy had called him Mr Mac.

They stood in the narrow hall. She could smell the wax polish off the coatstand.

'Ivy told me to tell you she'd gone out and would be back later.'

'Oh.' She was so tired and so dirty.

'I tell you what. I have a wee pan o' broth bubbling nicely. Why not come in and share a dish.'

Lizza hesitated.

'Come on now, ye can pay me for't at the end of the week when you get your pay. I can tell you now that Ivy'll have nothing up there.' His eyes watched her narrowly but there was no threat in them.

So she was hustled into the sitting-room that had more furniture in it than she had ever seen. High glass-fronted cupboards full of fancy china; a large sofa and fat padded chairs. Mr Mac pushed her into one of these beside the roaring fire. The height and the heat of the fire reminded her of her mother's careful stoking on a washday; too hot to sit too close. Mr Mac hustled off and Lizza's eyes alighted on a dresser standing in a recess beside the fire. The top half was full of shelves, and the shelves were full of books. She had never before seen so many books at once, in a house. The headmistress at school had had just such a cupboard, with the books gloriously inaccessible behind glass. But even she had not had that many books. She thought of school, and the hours spent in Miss Hesketh's room, saying speeches and declaiming poems. She thought of not wanting to go home, wanting to stay there in the calm herb-scented presence of Miss Hesketh. The fire was very hot and the chair was soft and comfortable, enclosing her aching limbs. She put her head back and closed her eyes.

She was having a hot bath beside the roaring fire specially stoked up by her mother. The heat was trapped in around her by the clothes-horse draped with a large grey blanket.

'Lizza. Time you was finished.' Her mother's voice came from the other side of the blanket, muffled.

She rubbed the small piece of soap over her hands, gritty from the day's work in the bobbin shop, enjoying the seeping heat that was taking the ache out of her limbs.

'Lizza, get out. Bernard'll be back soon.' Her mother's voice was very muffled but still urgent, demanding from the other side of the thick grey blanket.

'Girl! Girl!' There was a hard hand on her shoulder. She opened her eyes to the sight of Mr Mac's face above her. 'Better wake up now. Don't you know you've been asleep for more than two hours?'

She sat up and rubbed her face, remembering now what Mr Mac's voice reminded her of. A doctor who used to come to the Martindales'. He had been a Mac-something as well.

'I've heated your broth for you. Come and sit up for it.' A corner of the large chenille-clothed table had been set with an embroidered cotton cloth and silver cutlery winking in the light of a pair of gas-mantles now lit above the mantelpiece. She looked at her hands.

'Can I wash my hands?'

'Certainly you can, girl.' She was led through to a small scullery, with shelves neatly stacked with dishes and pots, and an impressive gas stove. Mr Mac put a bowl in the brown glazed sink and half-filled it with water from the single tap. He topped this up with water from the kettle that was humming and simmering on the stove. Then he left Lizza to wash her hands and face, and smooth her hair back with the brush and the comb which had been a present from Bea. The embroidered bag had not left her side all day.

'That's better.' Mr Mac was sitting up to the table with a book and a magnifying glass. She sat opposite him and waited to eat. She had never in her life eaten at a table without someone saying a prayer first. 'Come on, girl. Something wrong with it?' There was a cross note in Mr Mac's voice.

She thanked God in her head and ate the broth and the

plate of bread which accompanied it, in silence. He turned
the pages of the book and peered at it with the aid of his
magnifying glass. When she had finished she put the soup
bowl on to the empty plate.

'Can I wash these up?'

He looked up through his round glasses. 'No, you
cannot. I wash my own things, then I know it's done
properly. What you can do is take the dirty dishes into the
scullery and make a pot of tea. It's all ready.'

Which it was. The simmering kettle, the warm teapot
beside it with the tea in it, and on the table a tray with two
cups and saucers.

'Oh. Just the job.' He closed his book, put his magnifying glass on the top, and put it to one side. She poured him
a cup of tea and passed it to him. She poured her own and
then passed him one of his own biscuits. There was a
silence as they munched away. She felt pressed to say
something.

'You have a lot of books.'

'Yes. Some of them were my father's. Schoolmaster, he
was, in Perth. When he died his books came to me. A great
treasure, they are, with so much time on my hands. But
it's not easy. I can't see so well since the war.'

'I have a book.'

'Have you now.' There was a grim smile and a mocking
in the tone. She had heard so many variations of that tone
in the last two days.

'Yes, I have.' Crossly she fiddled with her embroidered
bag and slammed the book on the table.

'Temper to match your hair, I see. Here, let's see.' He
pulled her Shakespeare across, peered at it, then picked
up his magnifying glass for a closer look. 'Oh. I see now.'
His tone was still mocking. 'And do you know any of it.'

'Well, only *Henry V* and *Julius Caesar* by heart, but a lot
of the main speeches in *The Merchant of Venice* and *The*

Tempest, and bits and pieces in the other plays. And a few sonnets, of course . . .' She purposely kept her voice light.

'Touché, as the French would say! I apologise for my mistrust. What's your favourite speech then?'

'I don't know. I like it all. Maybe Portia in the Court-room.'

'Can ye say it for me? I tell you what. Portia's speech is the price of the broth.' There was no mockery in his voice and his eyes were less cold now. She trusted him.

'All right! But I have to stand up.'

He nodded and she stood beside one of the high padded chairs near the fire, one arm on the back.

> '*The quality of mercy is not strained,*
> *It droppeth . . .*'

There was a noise and clatter outside the door, shrieks of female laughter and lower, male, cajoling terms. There were bangs on Mr Mac's door. He stood up, his face tightened back into the bitter shape she had first seen. He pushed her book across to her and she stuffed it into the embroidered bag. He opened the door and Ivy fell in. It was as though they were handling secrets.

'Now, Mr Mac. Where've you been hiding my little sister? Oh, there you are, Lizza. I hope you haven't been bothering nice Mr Mac.'

Lizza looked at her sister. Her face was flushed and her lipstick was smeared outside the proper line of her mouth. She swayed slightly as she stood, a faint smile on her lips and her eyes glassy, with little expression. The shadowy figure of Gilbert was behind her. Lizza wondered what her mother would think if she saw Ivy like that. She would belt her within an inch of her life with Bernard's pit belt. Lizza, standing there, felt like doing the same. With her fringe and her loud voice and the smell of violets and gin and smoky taverns she had spoiled something good. A hand in her back pushed her forward.

'You get yourself up to bed, girl. It must be far past your bed time!' Mr Mac's voice was grim. 'I just want a wee word with your sister.'

She flew up the stairs three at a time, passing Ivy's door and going straight to her little room. Light filtered in from the gas street-lamp outside. She turned the key in the lock, then slowly stripped off her clothes and put on the night-gown her mother had packed for her. Then she brushed her hair a hundred times with Bea's brush and jumped into bed. After ten minutes the door rattled gently, and she heard Ivy calling her name softly. She pulled the quilt over her head and didn't answer. After a few minutes Ivy went away and the silent night crept into her head and let her sleep.

5 *Letters*

In the next few weeks letters were lifelines for Lizza. She threw them out and caught hold of the replies as they were returned to her, keeping some kind of binding with people outside herself.

> 32 Conduit Street
> Low Moor
> Bradford
> 27th February 1926

Dear Mam,

I have arrived safely here. I have my own room on the landing above Ivy. The landlord is a man called Mr Macferson and he is kind. He cannot work as he was hurt in the war with shrapnel and gas. So he has the house and lives on the rent. I hope you are keeping well.

> Your daughter,
> Lizza

P.S. I enclose the letters for the others inside this envelope to save money.
P.P.S. Ivy says to give you her regards.

Dear Bernard,

I am writing small to get a lot on this one sheet. I hope you are well and everything is all right at the pit. I miss seeing you and the girls and Mam of course. Ivy's not much good to talk to. She has a night job as well as a day job and is out a lot. Mr Mac, whose house it is, is in all the time, because he has a bad leg and bad eyes from the war. He has told me some of the things that happened, and I couldn't believe it. Fancy our Dad going through all that. Mr Mac says that he sometimes wonders what they fought for when he looks at the mess we're in now. Bernard, he knows all about the mines and the strikes in '21 and that. Fancy, living all this way away in the middle of the mills, not a pit in sight. He says the miners have a just cause and should fight to the bitter end.

But that's not the best thing, Bernard. The best thing is, you should see his books. A whole bookshelf of them. Shakespeare and Milton and lots of history and geography. You can get lost for hours in there. And he seems to know every single one. I'm in there a lot (with Ivy being out) either reading or talking. Sometimes I say the poems or the speeches for him. Sometimes I don't always like that because it reminds me of being at home too much, with you and the girls.

Work's not so bad. I work with a lot of old women, like clucking hens. I clean up and clear away a lot. Sometimes I cry because I am tired and because I wish I was at home. I don't let our Ivy see. She's different Bernard, different from what she was at home, but somehow the same. I don't think she's too pleased I'm here, now I'm here.

Write soon, Bernard. I miss our talks.

Your loving sister,
Elizabeth Bremmer

P.S. You should see the height of the chimneys here. Clustered against the sky like still families.

P.P.S. The journey was all right. I saw a lad on Durham station who was getting passed from one man to another like a misplaced parcel. He had run away from some school I think, and they were sending him back. The funny thing about him was he had snow-white hair, nearly like a moth's wing. You'd feel it'd glow in the dark. The train was really fast and I met a nice family. They had this funny little girl who clung to me like glue. They asked me to call and see them one Sunday. I think I will. Ivy's out nearly all Sunday and Mr Mac's very gloomy on a Sunday. Something to do with him being Scottish, I think.

32 Conduit Street
Low Moor
Bradford

Dear Mr and Mrs Bamburgh,

I hope you arrived safely back home after your train journey. I enjoyed the journey, it being the first time I was on a train. I had not realised we would go so fast.

I am now staying at the above address with my sister Ivy and her husband. I did not realise that she was married until I arrived. I have a grand little room under the roof and at night I can see the stars through the window as it is too high for a curtain.

I hope Iris is well and the twins. They were nice to talk to on the train. I would like to thank you all for your pleasant company on the train. It was very nice, it being the first time I was on a train.

I have a job in the bobbin shed at the mill. The women here are very kind, especially Mrs Cobbett who's a kind of forewoman. The women in the weaving sheds themselves are a bit hard on you though. One day I was waiting for our Ivy and a whole crowd came around asking who I was, what my name was, pushing me from one to the other and pulling at my hair and calling me Red and Redlass. Well you can tell the twins I thought of Horatius at the bridge and I gave them a good kick. (I was wearing a pair of clogs given me by Mrs Cobbett.) Well, I think they were so frightened that they just stook back and started to wander away, pushing and knocking each other with hoots of laughter and shouting back bad names to me. Anyway, they've not bothered me since. The women in the bobbin shed are nicer.

> Yours sincerely,
> Elizabeth Bremmer

71, Fendale Street

Dear Lizza,

It was grand to get your letter and know that you were safe arrived. I am pleased that you sound fairly settled, though you are bound to have some difficulty at first. Take no notice of Ivy if she is a bit funny. She always was a bit funny, wasn't she? Can you remember the time she went up to the town in boys' clothes with her face blacked up? And when she put frogs through Mrs MacLaughton's window? And when she locked herself in the bedroom for two days and I had to creep in through the window while she was asleep? Maybe it's a good thing you don't see too much of her!

It sounds as though your landlord is a decent man. He is obviously keeping his eye on you. Maybe it's not

such a good thing if you spend too much time with him.
Have you no young friends from work?

The business over the pay is getting worse. They are
unyielding, waiting for us to give in again. Wanting
more work for less pay. I don't know whether they live
in the same world. There's no question that action must
be taken. If we give in now we'll be back in the dark
ages. Is there any talk of a General Strike where you
are? They talk here about it, saying that it's the only
way to get mine owners and other bosses under some
control. They talk here about it but don't organise it
much. There was this bloke called Jack Crill talking at
the lodge, talking about the significance of organisation. How the side that was best organised would win in
a General Strike, and that communication and control
of food would help us get justice. He asked for any local
volunteers to help with the communication network,
and I volunteered. I have to go to a meeting in Durham
next Saturday afternoon to listen to how they intend
doing it. The lads here say it is useless bothering on like
that, and the T.U.C. will organise it nationally. But
what this Jack Crill says made sense to me. Not much
difference to me, between wanting the T.U.C. to do
what they like and letting the bosses do what they like.

Anyway, other things are happening. Ma says that I
have to tell you that poor Mrs Donahue died. She was
down helping on the farm a couple of bitter cold days
last week. Came home perished with cold and died the
next day. Her funeral was on Wednesday and all the
street was there, though it was a poor plain wooden box.
Ma baked and poured the tea for all the people who
came. Jack Donahue was like a man off, hunched in a
corner as though a breath of air would blow him over.
Various relations scooped the children away, I don't
know whether they'll stay with them. Ma says they may

have to go to the Home. She's upset over the children more than anything. She was never close to Mrs Donahue but she always worried over the children.

Our Johnny has settled at school now. Never had the cane for at least a fortnight and is top of the class.

I will finish now as the light is fading but I am looking forward to hearing from you and all your news. Ma says to send you her good wishes and I too send good wishes from,

> Your brother,
> Bernard

Dear Lizza,

A little note to you in Bernard's letter. I hope you are as well as you sound in your letter. I worried about you as you were so little there getting on the train. I cried all the way back to the house and the missus made the cook make me some tea. That was really nice, on the chair in the hallway too. Our Bea sends her best and will write to you in Bernard's next letter. She's seeing a young man now, can you believe it? He works in the next shop and is a lovely dancer but quite a flirt. Even charms Ma when he comes; now and then she smiles and laughs at him. There's a friend of Bernard's who waits around a bit for me, but I don't know whether I really like him. Anyway it seems a bit daft somehow, me having a young man. Our Bernard's dead mixed up with the men at the pit. All manner of folk coming and he gets more of a misery every day. Something's definitely up.

Bernard says he told you Mrs Donahue died. Ma says she was only twenty-five. Wouldn't you say she'd be twenty years older than that? I think her husband's gone crackers altogether now. Sits on his hunkers at the back gate watching you go backwards and forwards, his eyes so closed you think he'd be asleep. Even worse, twice he's been walking on the back street as I've come in from work. And do you know he kind of fell against me as he passed me, then got hold of my arm and looked me in the eyes and said 'Sorry, Bea,' then stumbled off. Gives you the shudders. If our Bernard weren't so busy I'd tell him. I daren't tell Ma as she'd say it was my fault.

I am going out now to see Sally Tippling who used to work next door to my work. She went away to Scarborough in service but is back now.

You take care of yourself and write soon.

> Lots of love,
> Renee

> 5 Thornlea Street
> Bradford

Dear Elizabeth,
Thank you for your letter. It was very nice to hear from you. Mr Bamburgh says you have a nice hand with a letter. The boys and Iris were interested to hear your news. Iris was particularly excited to hear about you and asked to see you.

Perhaps you would care to join us for tea on Sunday. Mr Bamburgh has drawn you a map to show you how to get here with details of the trams you might use. We look forward to seeing you. We have tea at four.

> Yours sincerely,
> Blanche Bamburgh

32 Conduit Street
Low Moor
Bradford

Dear Mrs Bamburgh,
    I thank you for your kind invitation and have pleasure in accepting it.

Yours sincerely,
Elizabeth Bremmer

At the same time as Lizza was writing and receiving letters, Roland King, who had seen and been seen by Lizza on Durham station, wrote two letters and received one.

School

Dear Mr Silkin,
    I write to thank you for the kindness shown to me in taking me back to Durham, and to ask you again not to write to my father. I feel that the whole matter would worry him too much, and he is in no position to do anything.
    Thank you again, and I would like to send my best wishes to Mrs Silkin, whose kindness at my mother's death always stays in my memory.

Yours sincerely,
Roland King

P.S. I am having to ask a maid to post this, private letters are forbidden. R. K.

School

Dear Father,

Thank you for your letter of the 15th. South America sounds very exciting and seems a thousand miles away from here.

Not much happens at school but there is talk among the boys and some masters of a National Strike. They say that it is about Bolsheviks and revolution and a threat to Britain's sovereignty. The miners in this region are, according to the teachers, particularly militant, but I wouldn't know. They may be all around us but all we see is boys and masters and the people at the Cathedral. So Bolsheviks they may be, but invisible Bolsheviks to me. It seems very far away to the day when I, like you, will be at sea, free and under the sky. I remember that you once told me that you were fifteen when you first went to sea. That's a year less than I am now. Is there no chance that I might start earlier?

Your loving son,
Roland

49 High Street
Bishop Auckland

Dear Roland,

I write to tell you that I have, this last time, decided against writing to your father. Mrs Silkin and I understand and sympathise with your predicament but earnestly beg you to remain true to your father's wishes and benefit from the excellent education he has provided for you. Above all I urge this. Whatever you do, whatever your future plans, you must make sure Mrs

Silkin and I are privy to them. Otherwise we are forced to fail our avowed duty to your dear parents, to whom we have been very attached.

Yours faithfully,
Amos Silkin

Roland read these words with a feeling in his stomach as though there was a great hand there, clenching and clenching. He was sorry about Amos Silkin but he knew his feelings would make him run again, no matter what his head or his commonsense said.

6   Out to tea

Mr Mac lent Lizza his watch for her journey to the Bamburghs'. He was concerned that she didn't miss the two trams the journey necessitated. She told him she was sorry she would miss their usual Sunday tea and currant buns, the half-hour between six and six-thirty which they shared on Sunday.

'Oh, go on with ye. It'll be a nice change for you. You do need some younger people around.' He pushed her shoulder rather hard, a funny gesture. 'What about Ivy?'

'She's gone to work at the pub, so she's not bothered what I do.'

'And 'll be back the worse for wear wi' that useless man of hers.' His face was sour. 'How she comes to be your sister I canna tell.'

'She's all right, Ivy. Just goes her own way. Always has.' Lizza tucked the heavy silver pocket watch into the embroidered bag. 'Don't worry about your watch. I'll take good care of it.'

She skipped down the road in her new green leather shoes, a bright green scarf round her neck cheering up the navy coat. Her mother used to say, 'Blue and green should never be seen,' and it drummed through her head as she danced along. The pale green wool dress lay smoothly under the coat. As she had handed over the seven and sixpence for the dress in the bargain shop, it crossed her mind that Bea earned less than that for a whole week's work. The toil in the bobbin shed, even the shouts and cuffs of the mill girls, were a fair penance, she thought, for such an advantage. She only wished that Bea could see her. Bea would have loved her in green and was always generous with her praise. She imagined the physical crunch of one of Renee's heavy cuddles, and her stomach clenched and the dreaded tears welled in her eyes again.

One tram took her into the centre of the town and she caught a second one out to Fenton where the Bamburghs lived. There were quite a few people out on this bright Sunday, families with scrubbed children, fathers and mothers in their Sunday best, young men and women out separately in pairs but interested in each other, sidelong glances and deftly aimed twigs drawing discreet attention and responsive giggles.

Through the tram window the high industrial and commercial buildings gave way to well-packed living streets scattered round with people leaning on doors, squatting on door steps. Here, children clustered in a variety of groups, patched and soiled, sometimes barefoot, not quite as shiny as the children inside the tram. Soon the houses became more individual, the doors large, the paints dark but clean, set within small dark gardens defending against passers-by. In this area no one stood on doorsteps, but white lace curtains twitched here and there as the tram clambered past.

At the terminus the only people to alight were Lizza and an old woman with a thick coat and a black hat planted firmly on the front of her head. Lizza turned to help her get down from the tram and received no thanks. Getting Mr Mac's watch out of the embroidered bag she saw it was still only three o'clock.

She looked at Mr Bamburgh's carefully drawn map which showed her how to get from the terminus to his house. It was very clear. She went off down the road indicated, noticing as she went how the houses became more and more separate from each other. First eights, then fours, then twos, then houses standing on their own in dark gardens.

Here again were people walking in twos and threes. You know they're not going to work, thought Lizza. They have a Sunday look, a work-free fashion. The men with hats and canes. The women and even small girls with hats, the boys with soft caps over stuck-down hair and fat necks in collared shirts. She thought of poor Mrs Donahue, now dead. I wonder if her children did go into the Home. It really was a nice hat even if I didn't know then. Smart, and with that mouse-like felt. Flying from my head like a bird, me being sick from the train. Dark green velvet with a feather. That's what I'll get. Next pay day. Mrs Donahue would have liked that. Irish green. There is a green hill far away without a city wall, where the dear Lord was crucified, who died to save us all. 'Sorry!'

The tears in her eyes had blinded her briefly and she bumped into a tree on a corner. Saying sorry to a tree made her laugh and she referred to her map again. Maple Avenue. This was it. The house was called Meadow Lea. She could see it four doors from the end, quite new with a tall stone porch and great stone-framed windows on each side of the door. There was a green hedge round the square front garden and a green glossy bush beside the door. Lizza took out the watch. Three-thirty. Too early. She turned and walked nearly back to the terminus, then walked slowly back again.

By the time she got back to the corner, it was two minutes to four. She waited until the pointer said one minute to four then, steady and stately, walked to the big brown door. There was a brass knob marked 'Bell' in the stone to the right. She pushed it. There was no give. Then she pulled it and the ball seemed to come away in her hand. She heard a ringing in the house as the bell-pull slid slowly back into its rest.

Two heads appeared at the window on her right. The twins were grinning and waving away at her. She smiled back then composed her face as she heard someone opening the door. A small girl with a flat face, black dress and white apron opened the door wide, cocked her head enquiringly.

Lizza was at a loss. 'I'm . . .' She couldn't say Lizza. What did you say? 'Mrs Bamburgh?'

'Yes, that's right. Are you Miss Bremmer?' The sharp eyes were taking in the thick coat and the hatless state. Lizza thought about Renee and how gleefully she would have told the tale of such an inept visitor when she got home. She put her chin in the air and gave a big smile as though the girl were Renee.

'Yes. Mrs Bamburgh . . .'

''S'pecting you. Come in.'

She walked past the girl into a broad hall which had a red and blue glow from the coloured glass in the door. There was a smell of polish and a sweet perfume of flowers that she did not recognise.

'I'll take yer coat.' The girl held out her hand for it. Lizza took it off and noticed a change in the girl's eye when she saw the green dress. She thought the girl recognised a stylish dress, but perhaps she was recognising it for a seven and sixpenny bargain. She handed her coat to the girl, smiling again.

'Thank you. What's your name?'

'Dora.'

'Thank you, Dora.' She felt at home with this girl, as though Renee were near. A big door on her right opened and the fluttery figure of Mrs Bamburgh emerged.

'Elizabeth. How nice to see you. I'm glad you found your way.' She came over and laid a soft hand in Lizza's and almost pulled her into the room. Dora, the maid, shut the door behind them with a heavy thump.

Mr Bamburgh, standing with his back to a bright fire, nodded and reached out to shake her hand. Iris, sitting very prettily with an open book on her lap, looked up, then pushing the book to the floor, stood up and put her hand out. Lizza, not knowing what to do, shook it, but Iris would not let go.

'There, Elizabeth. I told you Iris particularly wanted to see you.' The boys were wriggling from foot to foot, bubbling with repressed energy, waiting for her attention.

'Hello,' said Fergus. 'You goin' tell us some stories?'

'Stop, stop,' protested Mrs Bamburgh. 'There will be plenty of time for that. Sit down, won't you, Elizabeth. You must be tired after that long walk from the tram.'

She sat down on a padded but rather hard sofa, answering questions from both Mr and Mrs Bamburgh about her work and her life. She answered automatically, her mind busy with other things. Iris really was like Emily Sargent. She too was clingy and strange and unspeaking. Poor Emily walked, or fell, into the colliery pool one night and that was that. Lizza had cried at her funeral, feeling a great loss.

Lizza looked at all the eager faces looking at her with expectation, as though she were a good meal and they were just about to eat her. Really, she'd be more at home in the kitchen with Dora. Nattering on and pretending she was talking to Renee. The boys are lively enough, she thought, a bit like two sides of Johnny. But Iris with her pale face and eyes, now crowding beside her on the couch, was the most interesting to her. And, as she listened to the Bamburgh's polite questions, and answered them equally politely, she realised that Iris was the reason she was here.

At half past four Dora announced that tea was ready. The tea table was groaning with food, but as she ate Lizza was pleased to note that the drop scones were not a patch on Renee's and the cream horns had been bought in a shop. Her mother made beautiful cream horns, using greaseproof paper as a mould. They melted in your mouth. These stuck heavily to the roof of her mouth and she had to take a drink of tea out of the china cup to disengage the pastry.

Tea was eaten in silence only broken by Mrs Bamburgh's polite offerings of food to Lizza. A misfired crumb landed on Mr Bamburgh's lapel and he glared from twin to twin, then turned to his wife.

'Should we go into the sitting-room, and maybe Lizza will give us one of her excellent poems?'

The twins leaped up and were sternly ordered to sit down and leave the table with dignity. The party made their way across the hall, past Dora who was waiting to pounce on the debris. Her eyes moved sideways, watching Lizza as she passed, and Lizza wondered just when her working day would end. Maybe she should offer to go and help her. She hesitated. Fergus shouted at her elbow.

'Come on, Lizza. They're waiting.'

Waiting for what? She walked in and they all looked across at her. The broad bulldog face of Mr Bamburgh and the worried owl-like face of his wife, the blank doll face of Iris and the eager bird-like faces of the two boys. Mrs Bamburgh spoke, patting the hard couch beside her. 'Come on, dear. You're the guest of honour to-day. The boys have been dying to hear one of your poems.'

Lizza settled down, pulling the green wool smoothly over her lap. She thought of the letter she would write to Renee about singing for a supper. She looked at the boys, from one to another, thinking about Johnny. 'Well, I thought I'd tell you a tale about a great queen of the old times called Boadicea. My grandad and my mam told me this story many a time, even before I heard it at school and read it in the books.'

'A queen,' put in Johnson, 'a woman?'

'Aye. And she was very brave. Had red hair like me, which is why Granda told me the story. It was like this, see, she was a warrior queen and leader of her people . . .'

She watched the boys settling down on the stool they were sitting on and, at the edge of her vision, noted a similar relaxation in the adults. Bernard could do this, and her grandmother. Her mother had shown too, very occasionally in a hard and battling life, that she had this ability to make others see things through her own eyes, to draw them into her imagination to make them see and hear and feel things completely, which were only part of the story. She took the story through to its tragic and body-strewn end, and there was an audible sigh in the room. Not from one person, just a joint exhalation of breath that had been held at the exciting final stages of the story. There was a short silence, then an appreciative patter of applause.

Fergus looked up at her. 'That was really good, Lizza, really good. I bet that Boadicea was like you, a right fighter. Have you got another one?'

'Fergus, don't press Elizabeth.' Mrs Bamburgh's tone was unusually sharp. Lizza smiled at her. 'That's all right, Mrs Bamburgh. I have thought of another one.' She glared down at Fergus just as she would have glared at Johnny, in mock admonition. 'Mind you this is the last, the very last! It's a poem this time, or a bit of a long poem called *Beowolf*.' She went on to tell of the battle with the dragon and had another welter of appreciation to endure.

The others had prepared their own offerings. The twins tested everyone with a trick with a set of sticks and a box. Mr Bamburgh played some tunes at the piano and Mrs Bamburgh sang a sweet song about birds and springtime. Then Mr Bamburgh played a much jollier song about a sailor who found an island with lots of gold treasure. The twins loved it, and begged for more. 'No, I had this other idea, boys. I didn't want to be outdone by Miss Bremmer and her tales of heroism.' Mr Bamburgh took a battered red book out of his pocket, opened it at a marked page and stood with his back to the fire, one hand fingering his waistcoat pocket, and begun to declaim:

'*I see Barsad, and Cly, the Vengeance, the Juryman, the Judge, long ranks of the new oppressors who have risen on the destructon of the old . . .*' His voice gained strength as he went on declaiming the sad speech of the young man obviously about to die and somehow making the sad oration into a hymn of triumph, ' . . . *it is a far, far better thing that I do, than I have ever done; it is a far, far better rest, that I go to, than I have ever known.*'

Tears stood in Lizza's eyes and she clapped very hard to join the boys' appreciative shouts. She leapt up. 'Seven o'clock. I have to go, if you don't mind. I said I'd be back at seven an' I'm still here. Mr Mac'll be worried.'

'Mr Mac?' Mr Bamburgh's head went on one side. 'Mr Mac?'

'He's my landlord. Kind of keeps his eye on me. Me sister's very busy, see.'

'I see.' He pulled out his watch. 'Well, there isn't a tram till half past seven.' He leaned over and turned a small ornate wheel beside the fireplace. A bell clanged, and Dora appeared, rubbing her hands on her apron. 'Dora, run down to Mr Smithson, knock at the back door and ask if he would come with his taxi-cab. I know it's late, and a Sunday as well, but ask him as a favour to me.' Dora gave a sour look and a nod and turned on her heel. Two minutes later she was running down the road with a shawl over her head. Three minutes after that there was the roar of an engine outside.

The boys ran to the window. 'Here it is.' Lizza peered through with them; a shiny taxi stood at the neat gate, coughing and roaring, making a lot of noise. Dora leapt out and was soon in the hall again with Lizza's coat over her arm. Lizza thought again about Dora's long day as Dora helped her on with her coat, whispering under the general hubbub which mostly consisted of cat-like yells from the twins and fluttering squeaks from Mrs Bamburgh, 'Nice time, you had?'

'Yes, thanks.'

'Where you from?'

'County Durham.'

'Oh.'

'Well – er – Lizza. It seems that our Iris enjoyed your company. Now, you must come again.' Mrs Bamburgh had moved across and put an arm round her daughter.

'Yes, Lizza. We would like you to come again. We have all enjoyed your company.'

Lizza was red, not liking all the attention. 'Thank you.'

'Next Sunday,' said Mr Bamburgh. 'Come again next Sunday.'

There was an odd hooting outside. The taxi-driver was impatient. She smiled. 'Yes. Thank you very much.'

It was only after she had waved goodbye and was rattling away in the taxi that she realised what she was doing. Sitting in a car! Wait till Johnny heard about this.

The taxi chugged and gurgled along at a speed which amazed Lizza. The changing scenery of the city, noted in such detail by her earlier in the day, flashed past at a great pace. The whole journey was an exercise in narrowing. The streets became narrower, the spaces between the houses became narrower, until there was no space at all. The light became a narrower strip at the top of taller buildings. Lizza sat back comfortably into the padded seats of the taxi, fingering the red leather-backed book that Mr Bamburgh had given her as she left. *A Tale of Two Cities* by Charles Dickens. That would furnish her bed-time reading for a week, till she saw them again. She wondered whether she should go. It had been an adventure today with all the new things happening, but she had a niggling feeling that the pressing invitation was because she was so useful to them. They found her entertaining like the Punch and Judy puppets she had seen in the back street at home. A man had come and set up his boxy theatre and performed to the delight of hundreds of children, magically drawn to the green. And she worried about Dora, who was so like Renee.

The taxi chugged to a halt. 'Here y'are.' It was the first time the thick-necked taxi-driver had spoken. He turned and looked at her with curious eyes. He didn't have many fares to drop off in this district.

'Thank you,' she smiled, aware of his curiosity. She nearly tripped over the cluster of children who had gathered round the vehicle, rarely seen in this street.

'There you are!' Mr Mac's face was black and angry as he stood in the narrow hallway.

'Sorry I'm late, Mr Mac. Really, the time went away.'

'It's not that. That sister of yours. Or rather that husband of hers.' He turned on his tail and mounted the stairs. 'You'd better come and see. Prepare youself, girl. Prepare yourself.'

The room shared by Gilbert and Ivy was a wreck, no single piece of furniture was the right way up, all that could be broken or torn had been. The mattress was off the bed, and sprawled across it was Ivy, her head on one side and her arms and legs spread out, clumsy and ungainly.

'Ivy!' She was on her knees. She could smell the mixture of violets and gin that she'd come to associate with her sister. There was a purple weal down the side of her face, and fresh red bruises on her neck and the upper part of her arms.

Lizza put a kind hand to her face and the sharp grey eyes opened.

'Lizza?' Then her eyes closed, the blue veins showing through the fine white skin.

Mr Mac's hand pulled her on to the landing and he shut the door with a distinct click. 'See?' His voice was hard. 'Both came home the worse and he breaks up the place and her too.'

Lizza was black, dark inside. 'Mr Mac, I thought she was dead.'

'Would have been if I'd not come up here with my stick.' He was grim, angry.

Lizza cried for the death of the nice day, for her poor bruised sister. Mr Mac led her down and let her make him a cup of tea. When she brought it on the neat tray, he took out his pipe and looked at her.

'They'll have to go, girl. I can't have that. Not in my house. Plenty of people want rooms.'

'But Mr Mac, he's hurt her. She's all bruised. She can't go like that.'

Mr Mac rubbed the side of his leg where the shrapnel had gone in. His face was hard.

'I tell ye I'm not having folks behaving like animals under my roof. I never did trust that Grant feller, sly and shady with it. It was only 'cause Ivy knows – er – how to use her charms that I let him come. Mistake. I knew it at the time.'

'But . . . Ivy.'

'Of course, she could stay. If she were on her own. But not him.'

Lizza clung to that. 'Yes. She could stay and I'd take care of her.'

Mr Mac smiled crookedly and stood up. 'Well, that we'll have to see. In the meantime, we'll have to straighten that room and make your sister comfortable.'

They worked in silence for almost an hour, setting the furniture upright, and sweeping up the fragments of glass and pottery that littered the floor. They heaved the mattress, with Ivy on it, back on to the bed. She moaned and muttered but didn't wake. When they had finished Mr Mac stood staring out of the window. Lizza got a bowl and some water and started to clean off Ivy's face, washing away the specks of dried blood and the dirty grease that seemed to film her face.

Mr Mac coughed. 'I'll away down and make some tea and we'll see if we can get that in her. She shouldn't lie in that state all night.'

Lizza went up to her room and brought another pillow to prop Ivy up, went over her face again and timidly brushed back the black hair from Ivy's face. Without make-up, and with her cheeky fringe brushed back, Ivy looked much younger, prettier, even with the ugly bruise. Ivy started to struggle against the invading brush and suddenly her eyes opened.

'What yer doin' Lizza? Leave off.' She looked round the room, now rather bleakly tidy. 'Oh.' She remembered. She took the brush from Lizza's hand and absently started to brush her hair herself, teasing back the fringe. She looked round the room. 'D'you do this yourself?'

'No. Mr Mac helped. He's mad, really mad, Ivy.'

'Oh. He'll be all right.'

'Ivy. He says you've got to go. He's not having any more of it, he said.'

'Did he now?' Ivy's tone was mocking and there was quite a long silence after her confident statement.

'What happened, Ivy?'

'Well, Gil got mad at me. Sometimes does.'

'Why?'

'Well, he doesn't like the attention I get down at the Gantry. And . . .'

'What?'

'Well . . . chucked me job in on Friday 'cos of a slight

disagreement with the chargehand. Only told Gil today. He went crazy. I told him it was up to him to keep me, anyway. Went crazier then.'

'No need to hit you like that. You're a real mess, Ivy.'

Ivy laughed. 'I'm a real mess – you should see *him*!'

'Anyway, Mr Mac seems really set on you going.'

'Don't worry about Mr Mac. I'll see to him.' Ivy put her head on one side and winked at Lizza, who felt confused, as though things were happening behind a gauze veil and she couldn't see them.

Lizza's confusion was relieved by Mr Mac coming in with a tray of tea. Ivy turned to her sister. 'Now Lizza, I think you should be getting to bed. You gotta get to work in morning even if I don't.'

Lizza stood up awkwardly, angry at being dismissed but not knowing what to do.

'Let the girl stay, Ivy. There's nothing she shouldn't hear.' He poured three cups of tea and gave one to Ivy, one to Lizza and, taking one himself, limped over to sit on a chair by the window. 'The point is, Ivy, you and that man canna stay here any more. It isn't the first time this has happened but you should know better when your own sister is around. I want you out.' He saw her glance at Lizza. 'The girl can keep her room. I wouldn't throw a young 'un out. But you and he – I want you out by the end of the week.'

Ivy laughed. 'You're suddenly very hard, Mr Mac. Didn't used to be so – moral and upright, if I remember. My little sister should be in the conversion business, I think.'

Mr Mac put his cup and saucer back on the tray, took Ivy's, half-empty, out of her hands but left Lizza with hers. He smiled gently across at Ivy. 'That's it then, Ivy. Tomorrow I want you out and I'll give you back your week's rent.' Limping, and carrying the tray very care-fully, he left the room.

Lizza stood up. 'Ivy . . .'

'Get out. Get out!' She threw the brush at Lizza and it struck her brow.

'No need for that, Ivy. It's you that's in trouble, not me.'

'Out! Out!' Ivy slipped down in the bed and covered herself with a quilt.

Lizza closed the door behind her and set off down the stairs to return the cup to Mr Mac. He took it from her with unfamiliar stiffness.

'You'd better get off to bed now. Early start in the morning for you, if not for your sister.'

She blushed, not really knowing why. 'Goodnight, Mr Mac.'

'Goodnight, girl.'

A short man, with a raw bullet-head and thick legs so bandy that he had a clear circle between them, clambered on to the bus in front of Bernard. There were women with heavy shopping baskets and a few men scattered around the wooden-slatted bus seats. As he walked down the bus he noticed a woman, dark tanned-leather face and greasy ringlets, with a rough basket beside her. In the basket were small bunches of flowers. Not daffodils that he had seen on the wayside barrows in Durham. These were pale flowers, faded, perfectly and delicately formed but almost without colour.

'Like the pretty flowers, do you? Last for ever, these flowers will. Everlasting.'

'Make them, yourself, did you?'

'Me?' she laughed, showing teeth only faintly brown. 'No! Only God makes'm like this. Sin against God to mek anything with such grace as this. Sell yer a bunch for a ha'penny. Sold many a bunch during the war for the women to send away to their men. Put'm in boxes and sent'm. Arrived fresh as they went. Thinkin' of home the men were, seein' the flowers. Last for ever, see. All I do is pick'm wild off the field and out of the hedges and let'm dry in my van.' She thrust a bunch almost into his face and he could smell the scent of human beings in smoky earth, living, rather than the sweetness of flowers in the field. It was strange; delicate flowers smelling of people rather than flowers.

He fished a halfpenny out of his trouser pocket, took the

bunch of flowers, and put the coin into her hand. A slight crease of satisfaction turned down one corner of her mouth as she tucked it into a sacking-apron pocket. Then, completely ignoring him, she glanced stonily out of the window at a blond, almost white-haired boy who was running for the bus.

Bernard made his way to the back seat and sat down, his leather satchel on his knee. He carefully placed the dried flowers on top. The bow-legged man, three seats in front, twisted round with a grin on his face.

'Why marra! Are ye goin' courtin'?'

Bernard's face burned. 'No, I'm not.' He had not thought why he should buy the flowers. 'They're . . . they're for me sister. She's away from home and a bit miserable.'

The knowing look on the other man's face faded a little. 'Nice thought, nice thought . . .' he broke off, interrupted by a clattering figure hurtling down the central aisle of the bus. The engine coughed and roared, there was a clank and squeak while the brakes were released and the bus drew slowly away.

The boy with the white-blond hair sat heavily down beside Bernard on the back seat, and promptly lay down so his head was on the opposite seat. The bus roared as it gathered speed. Bernard put his hand on the boy's shoulder.

'You all right, bonny lad?'

The boy stayed down, but looked up at him with pale bright-blue eyes, unusual in these parts. 'Yes. I'm fine honestly . . . I'm a bit dizzy, that's all.'

Bernard glanced out of the window. They were at the south crossroads leading out of Durham, towards the spring brown of fields pencilled in by hedges in the rising folds of land. The boy sat up.

'Sorry if I startled you.' His voice was smooth, the vowels round and complete. That was unusual in these parts, too.

'No. That's all right. Just wondered if you was ill or sommat.'

'No.' There was silence and they swung against each other as the bus started up the long bank. 'Are you going far?' the boy asked, politely enough, in that very clear smooth-toned voice.

'Brack Hill. I live there. Near Granton.'

'Do you work in Durham?'

'No. I've been to an area meeting. For the Union.'

He patted the leather satchel on his knee. The satchel had come back from France with his father's things after the war. His mother had given it to him when he started working for the Union, saying it had probably belonged to some Germans anyway. Could never be gracious, Ma, either in giving or receiving.

'Area meeting?'

'Yes. There's a lot of talk now about this action. The miners're likely to strike and mebbe the other Unions as well. We're working on contingency plans.'

'Contingency plans?'

'Ways of organising the country when everyone's on strike, and you can't move about and the bosses aren't supplied with their materials.'

'Isn't that like revolution?'

There was a cackle in front of them. The bow-legged man was leaning back over his seat. 'I'd watch it, marra, if I were you. Could be a pliddy spy from the government. Talks like one of 'em. Could be the next generation of pliddy aristocrats and capitalists.'

'I'm no spy. My dad's in the Navy. I'm still at school.' The boy went very red and turned to Bernard. 'Why're you striking then?'

''Cos they want to cut our wages and make us work for longer hours.'

'Tickets please!' The bus conductor, neat and silver-haired, was rattling his change.

Bernard bought his ticket and the bus conductor turned to the boy. He searched his pocket, going very red. 'I seem to have . . .'

Bernard said, 'Where are you going?' The boy hesitated then said the name of the village before Granton. Bernard got his ticket and wondered at his own profligacy. First the flowers; then this.

'Which school do you go to then?'

'I go to school in Durham. My father's in the Navy, and my mother's . . . not at home, so I'm at school, at boarding school.'

'Boarding school?'

'We sleep there and eat there. Stay there for a whole term.'

'Sounds like some kind of prison.'

'It is like some kind of prison.' Bernard was amused to hear his own words, his Durham voice mimicked by this smooth-voiced boy. Fifteen mebbe. Not much older than Lizza. They were both flung forward as the bus stopped.

'Oh no!' The boy's voice was sharp, desperate.

A tall, thin man and a much older boy had mounted the bus and were talking to the conductor. He looked to the back of the bus and pointed. The tall, thin man nodded and the conductor came down the bus.

'Come on, laddie, yer teachers want you.'

He sat tight. 'No.'

'Come on. Ye'll have to come.' The white-haired boy folded his arms. The conductor looked back down the bus at the man and his young companion.

'Isn't coming.'

'Oh, yes he is.' The young man walked down the bus and got hold of the boy's left shoulder.

'Come on, King. You'll have to face the music.' His other large hand came down to get his right shoulder, to drag the boy, and Bernard caught it in mid-air.

'No you don't.'

'Get your hand off me.' It was a very superior, patronising sneer.

'Get your hand off him.'

'I have a right. He's run away from school and he's in trouble.'

'You've no right if he doesn't say so.' Bernard's voice was rough and grim, and had the authority of years of work and responsibility, though he was only a year or two older than this tall, confident young man. Suddenly the blond boy stood up and carefully, with his fingers, loosened the other's grip.

'All right, Foxer. I'm coming.' He turned to Bernard and put out his hand. 'Thank you Mr . . .'

'Bremmer, Bernard Bremmer. It has been good to talk to you.' Foxer was already on his way down the bus, and the blond boy turned round to smile broadly at Bernard. 'I hope your contingency plans turn out all right.' He was abreast of the bow-legged man and he whispered: 'All power to the revolution,' in his ear, loudly so that Bernard could hear. The man gave a cross splutter and the boy was gone.

The women settled back again with their baskets and the conductor pinged the bell and the bus gathered itself to depart. Bernard twisted round in his seat to look out of the back of the bus. The thin man in tweed was stalking towards a stately Ford car. The boy called Foxer had the blond boy by the collar and was moving him with unnecessary force to the waiting car. Just like a gaoler, thought Bernard, as he turned round in his seat and passed his hand thoughtfully over last summer's flowers, long dead but still holding exquisite form. Maybe Lizza would really like them. He wondered how he could get them to her.

8   Being alone

Lizza looked in on Ivy the next morning on her way to work. She was fast asleep, her palm under her cheek, looking about twelve years old. Gilbert was there also, fast asleep in a chair with his head back awkwardly. He looked like a gawping fish. When she returned from work that night Ivy's room was empty, cleaned out of all the bits and pieces that escaped the great crashing row. She raced downstairs and knocked on Mr Mac's door.

'They've gone.'

'Yes, girl. I know that. Tried to persuade me again. Feller Grant tried to persuade me with his fists, but I had my stick by me. I did say, girl, that your sister could stay if he went, but they weren't having any of that. Very fond of each other for a pair that regularly knock each other about.'

'Where did they go?'

'Dunno. Ivy did say she'd let you know when they got settled.' There was a little silence and he coughed. 'Seeing as the room's empty now you can take it if you like. Cost you nine bob a week, with coal. Save me finding another tenant, and the rest of the rooms are taken anyway.'

'Nine shillings? I suppose I could pay that if Ivy's not getting my wages.'

'Getting your wages? She took your wages?'

'Well, yes. She gave me ten bob a week pocket money and took the rest for my keep, paid the room and everything.'

He snorted. 'Mm. Everything would be gin or mebbe beer for Grant I think.'

'Mr Mac!'

'All right, all right. I'll say no more. Just one thing. You'll be better off all round now she's gone.'

Better off? Lizza's face was red. Her eyes filled with tears which didn't spill over. Ivy wasn't much when you reckoned. Lizza saw her very little. But she was a sister, and being a sister somehow meant that she was Bea, or Renee in a way. She was her own. Now she was alone. By herself. She closed her eyes and saw, not Ivy, or Bea, or even Renee. There, painted irreducibly on the inside of her eyes, was her mother. She was smaller, slighter than usual. Her hair was scraped back in a smooth black bun from her full pale face. She was standing just outside the back door in a large, enveloping pinny, a mop in one hand and a bucket in the other. She was looking straight at Lizza, full of fight and intelligence rather than the resignation more usual in the women in her street. She put her hand out to her and Mr Mac grasped hold of it. She opened her eyes.

'You'll be all right, lassie. I know you will.'

So Lizza spent that night moving her bits and pieces into Ivy's room. She opened the windows to let in the cold night air, evacuating the sickly, sweet-scented smells, scrubbed the floor and carted the various bits and pieces of carpet down to the yard to beat. At nine o'clock Mr Mac brought her a tray of china ornaments – his mother's he said – and three books. They were Byron's poems, Southey's *Life of Nelson*, and *The Study of Celtic Literature* by Matthew Arnold. She stood them in a row on the small table beside her bed and laid Mr Bamburgh's red leather copy of *A Tale of Two Cities* next to them.

She read a chapter before she turned the light off, then sat there in the dark, feeling inside her skin the trouble and disturbance of the last few days. What would Ivy think of her sitting there in her room, in her chair. Where was Ivy?

She felt a hard lump of anger inside her. Ivy had not bothered to wait, even to say goodbye. Her face ached and she wanted to cry.

She thought of her mother's white face and severely drawn-back hair. She thought of the odd times she had been clutched, almost always by accident, to the hard-bound bosom. She closed her eyes and tried to imagine that now, putting her head on one side to mime the feeling of comfort. The tears were wet, running now on her hot cheeks. She cried till she was coughing and hiccoughing all at once, and finally had to put on the light and find a towel and wash her face in the covered bowl of water waiting for tomorrow. She got some paper, a pen and a bottle of ink and sat up at the little table near the window.

Dear Bernard,

Our Ivy left Mr Mac's today because he was angry at her quarrelling with this man Gilbert. He – Gilbert that is – had hit her and knocked her about. So she has left me here at Mr Mac's on my own. Mr Mac's all right. Nice and kind. But I don't know the other people who have rooms. They are like distant shadows. It's so quiet here, Bernard, and now without Ivy there is no one. Except for Mr Mac. I can't understand, Bernard, why Mammy wanted so hard for me to be away. Do you think I could come home now? It is really so hard here . . .

Tears had made blobs and blotches and some of the words she had just written were becoming indecipherable in front of her own eyes. She screwed the page up and put it in the last embers of the fire, watching while it bloomed up into a flame, illuminating the room, then dropped in black flakes on to the glowing cinders . . .

Alice Bremmer raked loose coals down from the cavernous fireback, on to the melting heat of the fire centre. She organised the generation of heat with an efficiency coming from a lifetime's practice, so that the side-oven would get to the right temperature. She had done this for as long as she could remember, as long as she had been big enough to handle the long fire-rake, at about the age of seven, on the Friday and Wednesday baking days. She stood staring into the smoking coal, not yet hot enough to take fire. She had loved to work like that alongside her mother and, as she grew older, taking a greater part in the ritual of stoking, mixing, kneading, testing, baking. By the time she was eight her mother had kept her off school to help on baking days. By the time she was ten she had left school altogether, too useful a hand in the household which contained six men, her father and five brothers, all miners needing feeding and clothing and sustaining. Now, in her household, Bea had become her right hand, just as she had been her mother's right hand. Bea had had to go to school till she was fourteen, but she stayed at home on washdays and baking days. Being a good scholar and ahead of her class, this was no loss to her.

The flames started to lick out of the smoking mass of coal, and she raked carefully to cover them with coal without dousing the flame. Of course, Bea was at work now, and wasn't with her mother on washdays and baking days. Even so, she helped with the ironing at night. The Friday baking, Alice delayed till teatime, so they could work together into the early evening. Alice had never asked Bea whether she would like to do it. It was just taken for granted.

The fire could be left now and she picked up a half-made shirt and went across to her sewing machine, under the window, behind the thick lace curtain. She put a seam under the foot to sew. As she pumped away with her feet at the treadle she remembered the joy she had when Dobsons first delivered the machine. The gloating feeling and the stroking of the new wood, the sense of mastery as she loaded the shuttle and threaded it into the machine. All the parts had been so glittering and new. The machine had clothed them all since she had broken a cardinal rule and bought it on hire-purchase just before the end of the war. Ten shillings down and three and six a week.

She thought of the grim miracles she had wrought on this machine. Coats into trousers, shirts into blouses, working aprons from those very same blouses when they had done their turn in that form. She knew how to dismantle a garment, turn the material and make a different, albeit smaller, garment which looked like new. She achieved this with the finish on her work which was always fine, and small embellishments like drawn thread work, crochet edging, or embroidery, which gave the new garments an identity of her own making. Bea was very good at these embellishments and between them they made sure that nobody from this house looked like the ragged hollow-cheeked children commonly seen in the back street and on the green.

It was the shoes that defeated her. She couldn't make shoes, so was dependent on hand-downs from her own mother, of shoes from her brothers and sisters – usually twice or thrice worn already. One bad winter she had obtained unusual bounty from her mother, who was forbidden by her father to expend anything on this outlawed branch of the family. The Co-op delivery cart had called with six pairs of brand new boots. She had been relieved, released from the worry of shoeing her six children through the hard winter. Renee had had hers on straight away, leaping about in the back yard, striking sparks off the stone flags, delighted at having something brand new, straight from a shop. The others had been variously pleased, except for Lizza. As the thick-soled boots tumbled across the scrubbed kitchen table, her face hardened and her head went down.

'You gonna try yours on, Lizza?' Bea had enquired from her position on the wooden bench, lacing hers up. .

'No.'

'Why not?' Alice's brief relief turned to anger.

'Why, they're not for us. They're boys' boots. We'll get laughed at.'

Renee was inside now, leaning against the back door, breathing hard from her exertions.

'No, we won't, Lizza. Most of the people we know have to wear boots in the winter.'

'You mean most people like the Callaghans and the Kellys. You've laughed at them before.'

There was a silence. Bernard had his fastened up by now and they looked fine on him. Johnnie had his boots on his hands and now stopped clattering them together. Bea looked anxious.

'You'll get those boots on, girl.'

Lizza stood up and smoothed down her skirt with the palms of her hands.

'I can't, they're boys' boots.'

Her mother's hand clashed hard into her face. She stood still.

'You'll get those boots on.'

She stood with a smarting cheek and an aching jaw and said nothing. There was utter silence, as though all seven people crowded into the room actually stopped breathing.

'Get to bed!' It was four o'clock on a sunny autumn afternoon and Lizza was ten years old.

'Get to bed!'

Lizza turned and stalked to the door in the corner that opened on a little staircase.

For the next three days she wasn't allowed out at all,

except to school, and each of the three nights she was in bed by six o'clock. After that, having lost the battle, Alice didn't refer to it at all. Lizza inherited a pair of winter shoes from Bea, which were walked off and worn out. Bea got Bernard to take them to a man at the pit who cobbled shoes on the side. He patched them up and Lizza wore them. They were patched and shabby but they were not boots.

Alice bit the thread and smoothed out the seam on the shirt. The attitude of the others to Lizza had always puzzled her. Lizza was defiant and broke the rules which the rest accepted and lived by. They didn't bother. Without actually being defiant themselves they humoured and protected Lizza from the hard wrath that had moulded them into good obedient children.

It had been different with Ivy. She broke the rules and engined like a termagant in the neighbourhood, and made them all uneasy. She, being the oldest, frightened them. Some of her rebellion was to play cruel and often meaningless tricks on them; some of Alice's attempts to punish Ivy had been because of tearful and bruised younger children. They, like her, had been relieved when Ivy had gone.

It was not the same now that Lizza was away. The girls talked about her and worried about her; what was she up to? Bernard looked more perpetually glum; she tried to put that down to the harrassing strike ferment that was all around them. The way in which they missed Lizza made her feel a guilt unusual for her. At the same time she was equally pleased to be without the niggling presence of the increasingly strange girl who didn't fit into her order of things.

She stood up. From the heat emanating from the heavy iron door she knew the oven was ready. She went into the cold scullery and picked up two trays of cakes and put them on a lower shelf and went back to get two large round

cherry cakes to put in the middle. She normally made one
cherry cake, but this week she had made two.

She was sitting down half-an-hour later, pinning the
collar to the shirt, when there was a rattle at the front
door. She jumped. Who could be coming to the front door
at three o'clock in the afternoon? The front door was never
used. Callers at the front door meant death, or strangers,
or both. She knew about that.

It was a short man with neat hair and a moustache and
a coat that was too big for him – as though, one day, he
would grow into it. She vaguely recognised him.

'Mrs Bremmer?'

She wiped her slightly sweated hand on her apron.

'My name is Herbert Chilton. I'm from the picture
house.'

'Yes.' That's where she had seen him. Bea had dragged
her there to see some silly men flickering about on a big
screen to roars of laughter. A bit silly, Alice had thought,
though clever enough in the first place to get the silly men
on the screen.

'I wonder if I might come in, Mrs Bremmer. What I've
got to say is a bit – personal-like.'

She went cold in a remembered way. This had happened once before. It must be Bernard this time. She
spoke calmly enough.

'You'd better come through.' She led him through the
unused sitting-room with its linoleum, its upholstered
chairs, and the harmonium in the corner.

'Sit down.' She gestured towards one of the chairs
drawn up to the kitchen table and sat down opposite him.

He coughed. 'Well, it's like this. We were showing some
newsreel like. From the war. You know, men in the
trenches and on manoeuvres, getting on and off transport
and that.' He paused.

'Yes?'

'Well, we showed it last Saturday and all this week and three different people have come up to me and said, "There's Jo Bremmer, large as life." Two or three sequences.' He fingered his soft cap. She stayed silent. He coughed again.

'Well, I was curious about this and wondered if you'd mebbe come down and see it.'

'When?' Her voice was even.

'Well, any time. Now, like. 'S'nobody there and I can run them easy for you.'

She stood up. 'Yes. I'll come now. If you'll just wait a minute – I've got cakes in the oven.'

She got a cloth and took out the two cherry cakes, now perfectly cooked, and put them on thick cloths on the table beside the smaller cakes that were cooling. His nose twitched and his eyes glistened slightly.

'You like cakes, Mr Chilton?'

'Well, you're obviously a dab hand, Mrs Bremmer.'

She wrapped half-a-dozen small cakes in a spotless rag that she took out of the drawer and handed them to him. He clutched them awkwardly and watched as she pulled on a thick coat, and pulled a small shawl round her head.

'Right,' she said, 'I'm ready.'

The picture house was a large shed with only two windows, at the far end, covered with rather greasy heavy curtaining. There were rows of benches and a screen on a kind of stage at the front. It reminded Alice of the chapel where they had had the meetings when she was a small girl, before they had built the grand galleried edifice where she worshipped now.

Mr Chilton put her in the middle of the middle row, halfway to the back of the hall.

'You'll be all right, Mrs Bremmer?'

She looked at him and he scuttled away clutching his

rag package of cakes. The one light at the back of the hall went out and she was left in darkness. There was a grinding and clicking and titles leapt up in front of her, talking about the Great War. Then flickering men boarding ships, with packs on their backs and springing steps, hustling together but so cheerful. They were so lifelike, so real, not like the silly capering men she had seen with Bea. She leaned forward and searched the faces, making them out and losing them as the film flickered on. They were young faces artificially aged by the spurious manhood of luxurious moustaches. Alice was looking for an older face. Jo had been thirty years old when he went and thirty four when he died. She was looking for an older face.

A title came up saying 'Mortar Attack' and the screen was full of sparks and flashing lights, explosions that lit up a skeletal tree, the wrecked edge of a farm building, the silhouetted shapes of men leaping bravely forward. There was no way you could tell who they were. Another title said 'Over the Top', and now you could see individual men in long trenches like giant potato furrows. Here they looked grey and puppet-like, their faces forward, not caring who was making the record accounting their doom. She wouldn't have recognised her Jo here even if he had been there. These men had the uniform faces of death on them. The next title was more descriptive, 'Helping Comrades at the Bandage Station'. This was tents and men on stretchers, the tidy images that would be allowed. One man was moving around with a pitcher in his hand, pouring something into mugs held out by the soldiers, sitting and lying in positions afforded by their various injuries. He was pouring awkwardly with his left hand. His right hand and arm were heavily bandaged.

Alice watched Jo laughing and joking as he moved through the wounded men. The film-makers had used his movements to show the various faces and attitudes of the men at the bandage station. Jo had always liked 'having a crack' with his mates and here he was, yards away from hell on earth, cracking on as though he was down the road waiting for the pub to open, with his friends. He finally turned towards the film-maker and, with his jug in his hand, made a humorous gesture of making a toast and Alice looked straight into his eyes. It was as though the drab greys and blacks of the film shimmered and melted into true colour. She could see the red glint in his hair, the sharp blue of his eyes, the dingy colour of the khaki. Then he faded back to being a grey stranger on a flat screen, to be followed by another title, 'So They Lived to Fight Another Day'. The flickering stopped and the light went on at the back of the hall. Mr Chilton, out of his booth, called across.

'Was that him, Mrs Bremmer?'

'Yes. Yes, that was him.' She spoke quietly and it just got to him as an assenting murmur.

''D'you like to see it again?'

Again the assenting murmur.

She saw it three times in all. Mr Chilton would have shown it for her fifteen times. He knew his apparatus presented miracles to his audiences, but this opportunity had awed him with its drama. They walked together to the double door marked EXIT with a printed card. He could see she had had tears running down her face, but she was calm enough now.

'Was he out there for all the war?'

'Yes. He was drafted on the day war broke out, being in the Territorials. He was killed six weeks before armistice.'

'Well, Mrs Bremmer, it was people like him who Saved the Day.' Mr Chilton tended to talk like the titles that flashed on his screen day by day and formed his life.

'It was a senseless waste.' Her voice was hard, not allowing Mr Chilton his heroics. He coughed and stood at the door, putting his hands in and out of his pockets like a child caught stealing.

'But you wanted The Kaiser Vanquished, didn't you?'

'Yes. But I wanted Jo back. And he didn't come back. Not any part of him. Just a parcel of rubbish and them saying they'd done what they could.'

Mr Chilton stood helplessly. He had no titles to deal with this. There was a silence which she finally broke.

'Do you know what, Mr Chilton? It seemed he was talking to me down there. Right to me. I could hear his voice saying, "Cheer up, pet. Cheer up old girl. Things'll get better."' Mr Chilton breathed more easily. 'But he doesn't understand, Mr Chilton. They can't get better, things. What's wrong with things is that he's not there.'

She stumped off, making Mr Chilton feel uneasy and not at all sure that his sense of drama had lead him to do the right thing. However, as the weeks went by he was increasingly sure that he had done the right thing. Every third week a very pretty dark-haired girl turned up at his booth with a spotless rag tied around half-a-dozen delicious small cakes. He always invited the pretty girl to sit through the performances. Bea enjoyed these cinema visits, liking most the dramatic romances that looked to her so real, so full of life.

Alice was sitting in the front room when Johnnie got in from school. She still had her coat on and was sitting on one of the hard-backed chairs in the front room.

'You all right, Ma?'

'I'm all right Johnnie. Just get yourself something and go on off to play.' She hardly looked at him. He went back into the kitchen, put a cake in his pocket and one in his hand and went off, whistling. She was still there when the girls came in. The kitchen fire was just in, a hollow cave with a crust of smoking, burning coal. Bea took one look at her, and left her and went into the kitchen to make up the fire, clear the table and start the dinner. Renee stood hesitatingly, by the couch.

'What's the matter, Ma?'

Alice looked up at her, rather distantly.

'I seen your Da. At that picture house, up on the screen. "Scenes from War", they called it. He was up there, as alive as you are standing there.' Renee moved towards her mother. 'You get in there and help our Bea with the tea.'

Alice drew herself back from her daughter and Renee clumsily withdrew to the kitchen. The two girls worked together in uncharacteristic silence, their hearts heavy inside them, the house heavy around them. They had the table set and the vegetables done when they heard the music. From the sitting-room came not the majestic sounds of the hymn tunes with which they were so familiar, but light sounds of music-hall tunes. Bea, being the oldest, could remember their father singing and capering about on his last leave, singing these same songs. They were silly songs with silly words. Very cheering. The whole house lightened up.

Renee popped her head round the door, and waited for a space in the music.

'Tea's ready, Ma.'

'I'll be in.' Alice nodded but did not smile and bent her head to play the last of Jo's tunes.

The next Tuesday night when Lizza got in from work there was a letter from Bernard.

Dear Lizza,

It's quite a while since I have heard from you and I do hope you are feeling well. Everyone here is fine, though Johnnie got a black eye fighting with one of the

Kellys. He wouldn't tell us what for so Ma gave him another good hiding. But he bounced back like a rubber ball. You know our Johnnie. A really strange thing has happened this week. They were showing a newsreel of the war at the Picture House, men in the trenches and on manoeuvres. Anyway, our Da was there on the screen. Ma went up to see it but I don't know what really happened as I was on backshift at the time.

Things are pretty bad here at work. The talk is all of a strike, a national strike, if the pressure to take less wages is being kept up. The men are desperate and see the owners as their enemy and the government as the owners' creature. These are desperate times, Lizza. You are best where there is some work and where at least you will be able to pay your way, although you are much missed here by your

> Loving brother,
> Bernard

Lizza settled down to her tray of tea and bread and jam and read the letter again. She thought of her mother left as a young woman with six children, and she remembered how, even as a child, she had felt the bond between her mother and father. The gaiety and charm and quickness of her father had left an imprint on her mind. These were qualities which existed in the family now only in Renee's sense of humour and in her own temper. Maybe she herself was like her father and that was why her mother wanted her away. But that did not make sense. That would surely be a reason to keep her close. She smoothed her hand over Bernard's letter. It was very comforting despite its sombre contents. Bernard, at least, was thinking of her.

The next day when she came back from work there was

further evidence of Bernard's thoughts. It was a large cardboard box with her name pencilled several times on the outside, and clumsily tied up with string.

Mr Mac told her that a man with an empty wagon had left it. It seemed he had delivered coal to one of the large depots in Bradford and Bernard had asked him to deliver the package.

'So I gave the laddie a pot of tea and a good meal. Thought he deserved it for coming out of his way.'

Mr Mac watched the girl tearing at a string, delighting at the shining face after the sombre looks of the last few days. She gabbled as she pulled at the string.

'Fancy, Mr Mac! Fancy! I never had a parcel, ever. Mam had one or two in the war, from me Da. Then there was the parcel of his things when he was killed. But she didn't believe that, Mr Mac. She never did believe that. And in the parcel, guess what? His spare boots and uniform and all sorts of odd things, crosses and watches, and a little leather bag. I wanted it for school, but she wouldn't let me have it – oh!'

The parcel was open and she dipped her hands in and pulled out a paper package. Inside, a little crushed but stretching out into the air, was a little bunch of pale, almost colourless, flowers. She put them to her face and could smell smoke and cooking food. She held them out to Mr Mac.

'Look, Mr Mac. Flowers. Queer, aren't they? So lovely, but smelling so strange.'

'There's more.' Mr Mac pulled away some more of the newspaper from the top of the box. She reached in and pulled out another parcel. In it was a blackened tin, inside which was the familiar brown and broken top of one of her mother's cherry cakes. The delicate sweet smell, composed of all the times she had ever eaten her mother's cherry cake, hit her senses. She put that on one side.

Another newspaper parcel contained a delicate cardigan of cream wool, knitted, she knew, by Bea. The last parcel held a small blue glass vase, with just a tiny chip out of the foot. One of Renee's found objects, the sweepings and sparkling left-overs of her working life.

'The kettle, the kettle!' Mr Mac firmly turned her towards his little kitchen. 'Would it be in order to eat some of this little cake?'

9   *Learning a new game*

The bowl of stew made a brown circle within the brown circle of the bowl on the white cloth. Lizza looked up at Mr Mac's pinkish face. She had been recounting an incident with Ivy. He had grunted and snuffled a bit and said nothing.

'Stew's really very nice, Mr Mac. 'S'nice of you to make it for me. Don't do it for the rest of your lodgers?' Her tone was questioning.

'Big enough to fend for themselves, them. You, being so young, need company as much as the cheap bit of broth.'

She chewed on her bread, thinking about Bernard.

'I'm nearly fifteen.'

'Yes, lass. Ye look all of that an' then some. Even so, when I was your age I was still at school, and slept every night in my father's house.'

Scarlet seeped into her cheeks. 'Well. I had to come away, you know. There was no jobs and no money. Things going from bad to worse up there.'

He made a clicking sympathetic sound with his teeth. 'Yes. I know that. And they'll get worse before they get better. Still, not yet fifteen . . .' He coughed and, moving away from the table, leaned against the high mantel for several minutes until he managed to suck useful air into his lungs. When he returned to the table the subject was ended. He picked up her empty dish. 'And what will you be doin' this afternoon?'

'Don't know. Need to tidy up my room, got some reading and letters to write. I love Saturday afternoons.'

'Nice rest after a hard week, eh?'

'I'll maybe call on Mrs Cobbett. She asked me to go. Drew me a little map.'

'Where d'she live?'

'Barraclough Court. Off East Road.'

'You want nothing going down there. It's all thieves and vagabonds.'

'Mrs Cobbett's not a thief or a vagabond!' she objected.

'I might more rightly say some thieves and vagabonds. Your Mrs Cobbett's likely not one of them.' He paused. 'Well, get yerself away if that's where you want to go. Make sure you set out in time to get back in the light. Thieves and vagabonds are more likely to creep out of the woodwork at night.' His tone was hard with annoyance, which was more for himself than for her. Here he was fussing like a mother hen over someone who had nothing to do with him.

'Right, Mr Mac. I'll be back in the light, don't you worry,' and she flew out of the room.

'Who's worried?' he muttered at the closing door, unheard by Lizza.

The journey to Mrs Cobbett's was the reverse of the journeys she had taken on two occasions to the Bamburghs'. The roads changed from the broad, respectable streets of houses like Mr Mac's (some of which, like his, had more than one family) into narrower ones. She moved from streets to sections where narrow alleys opened out into courtyards with houses facing into each other, round a hard-packed dirt square. People of all ages were sitting or leaning or standing near peeling front doors. Children played in the dust and dirt with tins of water and sticks, constructing small cities and rivers of mud. Lizza thought she'd never find her way, but Mrs Cobbett's neat map, peppered with names like Paradise Court and Sebastopol Buildings, led her faithfully to Number Seven Barraclough Court, and a pale green door with a narrow

whitened step that shone against the grey of the pavement.

She knocked hard. The curtain in the narrow window
twitched briefly and a second later the door was opened.

'Lizza. Why it's right good o'yer to come.' Mrs Cobbett's face beamed. 'I didn't think ye'd manage. Come on
in.' The door opened directly on to a small square room,
neatly but very sparsely furnished. Above the fireplace
was a framed black and white scene of George and the
Dragon. On the mantelpiece stood four photographs in
ornate frames. Lizza's eye took in the couch and a wooden
rocking-chair and a table covered with a chenille cloth
under the narrow window. The small fireplace had no oven
but a standing grid for pans above a very modest fire. This
fire looked very small to Lizza, used as she was to the large
fires at home and the bounteous provision of Mr Mac.

'Sit down, sit down. Let me get you a cup of tea.'

Lizza sat on the couch. 'There's no need for tea, Mrs C.
Really.'

Mrs Cobbett was already busying herself in the cupboard at the side of the fireplace, putting tea in a metal
teapot and pouring water from a tall enamel jug into a
small kettle.

'Well, truth to say, Lizza, I was just fancying one
myself. So you'll do me a favour drinking with me.'

The fire was built up, the kettle on, and two china cups
and saucers placed on the chenille cloth as she was
talking. This being done, she hobbled over to the rocker
and sat down opposite Lizza.

'Hey lass, you look right bonny today – no need to blush
at the truth, now. That's a right pretty dress, goes with yer
hair a treat.'

The green dress, carefully pressed, was still her pride
and joy, but she was embarrassed by Mrs Cobbett's
systematic, albeit admiring, scrutiny. To divert attention

she asked Mrs Cobbett about the photographs on the mantelpiece.

'Oh, those. Get me them down, save me legs.' Mrs Cobbett clutched the framed photographs clumsily to herself as she rehearsed the names of the people one by one.

'This one is my ma and da.' A very proper formal photograph of an old woman sitting on a seat and an old man standing bolt upright behind the woman. She was dressed all in black and the man had a foreign-looking square beard and a round black cap on his head.

'They came from Russia mebbe fifty years ago. My ma would never speak English, not till the day she died. He did, like. Worked on the dyeing as a boss in the end. So he needed to speak English.'

'Couldn't you talk to her, then?'

'Oh yes. I speak the old language. And there's plenty around who do in Bradford. A few families from the actual village where they came from lived near us.'

'Why did they leave Russia?'

'It was a bad time there for Jewish people.'

'Jewish? I never thought you were Jewish!'

Mrs Cobbett laughed loudly, the laugh pinging off the painted walls.

'Well depends what you mean. I am Jewish and I always will be, 'cos I was born Jewish. But, I'm not a part of the community any more.'

'Why not?'

'Married out, and they didn't like it.' She turned over the second photograph, and the light caught the face of a young man in uniform. 'Thomas Cobbett. Met him when I worked in a sweet shop in town. He worked at the Town Hall. Till the war, that is.' The corner of her mouth twisted and she shoved the photographs in the chair, picked up the kettle from the fire and hobbled across to the table to pour boiling water on to the dry tea-leaves.

'The war swallowed him up like it swallowed up all the other young men.'

'My dad got killed in the war.'

Mrs Cobbett brought Lizza's cup. 'Terrible waste. I know we had to beat the Kaiser, but what a waste.'

She picked up the two other photographs, of two young boys in round caps and knickerbockers. 'And this is Harold and Reuben. Sixteen and eighteen, they are now.'

Lizza looked round. 'Do they live here too?' It seemed very small. Mrs Cobbett laughed ruefully. 'Where do you think I'd put'm with one room up and one room down? Some people do bring up families in these places, like. No, they're in America with my sister and her husband. They took'm with'm in 1920. Seemed like a good idea – me, with no husband and no prospects of jobs for them.'

'America?' Lizza was shocked. 'Why, that's hundreds of miles away. Thousands. They must have only been ten and twelve.' There was an accusing note in her voice. Here was something much worse than her own experience. She remembered the broad stretch of the Atlantic on the map on the wall in the school.

Mrs Cobbett regarded her thoughtfully, taking no offence at the implied criticism. When she spoke her voice was low.

'Well, it was like this, Lizza. I had to make up my mind right quick whether they should go or not. My sister only has a daughter, you see. Her husband was going to join his father who was in business out there. Needed new hands, and you know, we like to have our family working.'

'I didn't mean . . .'

'Don't think it didn't break my heart to let them go. I dreamt of them every night for a year. After that, the dreaming stopped, but the heartache goes on and on. But, even so, my heart's lifted when I get their letters. They're doing right well, both o' them. Reuben is opening a new branch, and Harold is in a college of engineering.'

'I'm sorry you miss them.'

'Don't be sorry for me, girl. My heartache is the price of their new life and I'd pay the price over again.'

Lizza sat quietly fingering her china cup.

'D'you think all mothers feel like that?'

'Likely, Lizza, likely.' She stood up and replaced the photos carefully on the mantelpiece.

'Anyway, no more talk of heartache, on a good Saturday afternoon, Lizza. C'n you play gin rummy?'

'What's that?'

'Cards. A game of cards.'

'Cards? My ma called them devil's feathers. I can't gamble.'

'Not gambling, Lizza. Just a little game and we use the buttons out of my old button box as sixpences. Here, I'll show you.' She got a thick-looking pack of cards out of a drawer, and a brown tin with a hinged lid. She put them on the chenille cloth, and counted fifty buttons for Lizza, and fifty for herself. Then she pulled out a chair. 'Here, you sit here, and I'll sit beside you till you get to know how.' Lizza sat down willingly and soon grasped the principle. They played the game in a merry fashion for an hour and Lizza wondered how her mother could see this as blowing the feathers of the devil. It seemed innocent enough.

Lizza crashed through Mr Mac's front door at half past five. It was still light so she wasn't worried about his black looks.

'Hey, Mr Mac. What an afternoon. Guess what. I learned how to play cards. A game called gin rummy . . .' Her voice faded as she saw his face. His skin was very white and there was a purple weal on his brow above one eye, with a thread of red blood filming across its surface. He was leaning against the table.

'Mr Mac. What happened, what's the matter?'

'I been attacked, that's what's the matter. That fool came back, looking for me money.' He nodded his head painfully towards the corner where a dark figure was dumped like a bundle of rags. She squeezed her eyes in the gloomy space and made out the pale red hair.

'Gil!' She looked around. 'Where's our Ivy?'

'Aye, she was with him. As bad as him in her own way. Aye, I know she's your own but she's different. Like a tinder in a box of flint. She makes things happen and not good things at that.'

'But where is she, Mr Mac?'

He lumbered away from the table and collapsed into the fireside chair. 'Went storming out, shouting about the pollis. She says I've killed'm.' The reddened eyes looked up at her. 'Can ye see for me, lass? Can ye see if he is . . .'

Lizza's skin tingled and she could hear the beat of her heart in her ears. How would she know? She had once seen a dead rabbit of Johnnie's, stiff and open-eyed in the bottom of its cage. Its fur had even looked like cut-out cardboard. She breathed in the familiar, faintly stuffy air of Mr Mac's sitting-room and moved towards the corner. Gil was lying on one shoulder with the outside arm flung back at a restless angle. One knee was drawn up, the other stretched out. She knelt down and put her face towards his. His eyes were veiled by the lids. She could hear no breathing. A trickle of blood stained the space below his ear and there was a blue weal under his jawline. She reached out and touched his face. It was faintly warm. But it seemed that he did not breathe at all. She turned from her kneeling position to look across at Mr Mac.

'He doesn't seem to be breathing. I can't tell.' The strained high voice was not her own.

Mr Mac looked at her dully. His voice was very cold. 'Get one of those pictures.' He nodded at the mantelshelf. She picked up a small framed picture of an elderly man in magisterial black. Mr Mac's schoolmaster father in potent middle-age.

'Now put it near his face. If he's breathing, then it'll steam up.'

She did as he said, her hand shaking slightly as she held it to the dead-looking face. She waited for stretched-out minutes, then turned the glass front so she could see it.

'It's steamed up. It's all right Mr Mac. He's not dead.'

There was a powerful sigh from the huddled figure in the chair. 'Right then. Now lassie. Go through to my bedroom and there's a wooden chest by the bed. Get blankets from there and a pillow from the bed.'

She followed his instructions like an automaton, easing Gil's head on to the pillow and covering him with the clean fluffy blanket, cream not white. As she moved him slightly he was heavy. She felt sure, quite sure, that he was dead.

She sat quietly in the chair opposite Mr Mac, unable to say anything to him and unable even to catch his eyes, which were fixed on the blanketed figure. He ignored her.

After five minutes the high voice of Ivy pierced the muffled silence. The door was filled with Ivy in a red dress outlined against the black bulk of a policeman. He filled the doorway, cradling his helmet in the crook of his arm. His face was long, like a loaf, the bleak indentations of his nostrils being the only sign of a nose.

'He hit him, Mr Mogdan, right across the head with a great stick. An' killed him, he killed him . . .' her shrill voice broke as she saw Lizza in a chair. 'Here's my sister. She lives here. She'll tell you. Not right, it isn't right.'

Lizza stood up. 'It's all right Ivy. He's not dead. Look.'

Ivy was on her knees beside the blanketed figure. 'Gil,

oh Gil. Why d'you get into these clatters?' Her hands were on his face. 'Yes, yes.' She stood up and wiped her hands down her red dress. 'Makes no odds, Mr Mogdan. He's right bad here. And it's his fault.' She gestured towards Mr Mac in his chair without looking at him. 'The old lad's crackers. We were just here to visit me own sister and he went wild. Right raving mad.'

Constable Mogdan, used in these parts to minor quarrels where force got out of hand, coughed. 'Is this right, mister? Is this what happened.' His voice was soft, thought Lizza, too soft for a policeman.

Mr Mac didn't reply. There was a heavy silence. The fire crackled and the clock ticked. Lizza spoke up. 'No, it's not, Mr Mac wouldn't do that. He told me that Gil wanted money, was going to take something . . .'

'There! I told you, Mr Mogdan, how worried I was about me little sister being here in his charge. No knowing what happens.' There was something in her voice, a sneer, an accusation that reminded Lizza of the mill girls when they tried to bully her in that first week, commenting on her hair and her shape. She closed her eyes as anger and rage rippled through her. It finally fixed itself on her right hand, which drew back in a loose fist and crashed towards her sister's face. She had landed three blows before the policeman had pulled her away. He sat her on a chair on the far side of the table.

'Don't you move from there, you.' He turned to Ivy. 'Now, let's see how he really is.' He kneeled down beside the blanketed figure, pulling his cloak out of the way. He felt Gil's pulse. 'Yes. He's all right. Just out cold. You go and get a doctor to come and dress these wounds. Mebbe needs the hospital. He'll know.' Ivy looked from Lizza to Mr Mac to Constable Mogdan, suspiciously. 'Go on, girl. Do you want to help or not?' She ran off and the tension went out of the room.

Constable Mogdan sat down at the table and took a notebook out of his pocket. 'Now, Mr-er-Macferson, is it? You look as though you've taken a bit of punishment. What's your version . . .'

Lizza heard the mumble of voices, but not the words. She thought about Ivy and her sneering voice. Ivy mixed up here with the awful Gil, married or not married she didn't really know. Here, mixed up with all this mess. What would Ma think of this? She would think it was like a scene from hell. She would think they were all, Mr Mac and Constable Mogdan as well, doomed, lodged in some waiting-room for hell.

Some coal broke its shape in the fire and random flames licked up. The men's voices mumbled on.

Lizza was miserably unhappy. She felt smeared and slimed by Ivy's words. Her lovely day was spoiled. Mr Mac was there, with a purple weal on his face, unrecognisable and full of anger. She had felt, since she came into the room, his anger against her. Why should he be angry with her? What had she done? It was Ivy's fault. She spoiled, she smeared everything. But she hadn't always been like that, not when she was at home. This place, this place did it. At home she had just been a tomboy. Just naughty like a child.

She wondered if Ma ever thought of what she was sending her daughters to. No. She couldn't. She just saw it as work in a bigger village than Brack Hill. She had nothing in her head or her imagination to give her pictures of this place, teaming with people and machines and beer and poverty with no restitution of green fields. No, Ma would never have sent her here had she known.

She stirred, the two men were looking at her. The policeman had his pencil poised.

'I said might it possibly be the case that you were in collusion?'

'Collusion?'

'Yes. You agreed to be out to leave the way clear.' His voice was high, like a woman's.

'I wouldn't do anything like that. Mr Mac knows.' She was frightened. She looked across at Mr Mac. There was a silence, then Mr Mac shrugged.

'No. I'm sure the lass would have nothing to do with it. Not the same kind as her kin.' But still he looked at her with a cold eye.

'Maybe she's good at putting up a front.' The high voice persisted.

'I don't need to put a front up, Constable Mogdan. Mr Mac and I were friends and I would do no harm to him as he would do no harm to me.' Her voice was icy and echoed to tones of Miss Hesketh, her schoolteacher. It was only after she said it that she realised she had put their friendship into the past.

'Don't you be uppish with me, miss. There's places for naughty girls like you, you know . . .'

Lizza leapt to her feet, but Mr Mac spoke before she could say anything.

'Leave the lassie, constable. She's right, and she's all right. Just got tangled in something not of her making.'

He looked across at the girl shaking his head very slightly to stop any outraged response. 'Why don't you go to your own place, Lizza? You want nothing here with policemen and near-corpses.'

She looked at the loaf-faced constable. He shrugged.

'You might as well, I suppose. I know where you are.'

She flew through the door and raced up to her room. She flung herself on the bed. She started by hitting the bed with her fist and ended up by crying till no corner stayed in her where tears could hide. She heard doors opening and closing downstairs and the babble of voices.

Much later there was a knock on the door. She stood up

from the bed and opened it. Mr Mac stood there, but did not come in.

'They've all gone now. They've taken that Gil feller back home in a taxi. Doctor says he'll be all right. Policeman says there shouldn't be any charges. Six of one and half-a-dozen of the other. In any case, any charges would be against him for trespassing.' He sounded desperately tired, and the white bandage on his head almost glittered in the dusk of the landing.

'Mr Mac . . .'

'No, leave it, lass. We'll mebbe talk about it tomorrow. Get some sleep.' He turned and hobbled painfully downstairs.

She lay down on the bed and found that the dry well of her tears had filled up again and could gush forth with the original force.

10 Visiting again

Lizza was up early on the Sunday, tidying her room, organising her clothes into a wash-bag ready to take to the public washing house on Monday night. She went down and timidly asked a dour Mr Mac if she could borrow his iron. She spent an hour pressing all her other clothes, being careful not to over-heat the iron on the fire. The careful thoroughness of the action drove away, momentarily, thoughts of the night before.

Just before twelve o'clock she put on the green dress with a clean white apron on top and went down to have her Sunday dinner with Mr Mac as had become the custom. She chose a book of Shelley's poems from his shelves and began to read, sitting quietly while he bustled about. The front of her mind read the words of the poet, but the back of her saw the two of them in the comfortable cluttered room. She thought of Ivy's cruel words the night before. What was bad about this? Sharing meals and talking. She was suddenly uncomfortable. She stood up.

'Can I not do something, Mr Mac?'

'It's all in hand, girl. Everything's on. Nothing to do.' He limped over and sat opposite her. 'One thing you might do. Read me a new poem.' The bandage was off his head and his voice almost normal, just a little stiff, as was hers.

By the time they had chosen one, and she had read it three times and they had talked about it just a bit, the smells and bubbling sounds from the kitchen cued Mr Mac into action.

He called from the scullery: 'Are you off out again this afternoon?'

'Er, yes. Mr and Mrs Bamburghs'.' She was not sure how to tackle this. 'That's if you don't mind.'

He brought in a dinner plate laden with three vegetables, Yorkshire puddings and a great slab of meat. He put it down in front of her.

'Nothing to do with me. You go where you choose. Nobody's in charge of you.' There was ice inside her at the bleak words.

Their dinner was a polite and business-like affair that made the food taste like salt in her mouth. After dinner she went straight up to her room and wrote a letter to Bernard. She had a stamp and would put it in the post-box on her way to the Bamburghs'.

Sunday night

Dear Bernard,

Thank you for the letter and the parcel. The flowers were really lovely, but strange as well. They smelled of fine tobacco. Can you remember:
"The odour from the flower is gone
Which like thy kisses breathed on me,
The colour from the flower is flown
Which glowed of thee and only thee."
Funnily enough I was just reading it to-day with Mr Mac.

The parcel came when I was feeling really left out here on my own and very black about it. Mr Mac enjoyed Ma's cake, and tell the girls their things are lovely too, and very useful.

Work has been all right. I'm more used to being on the go all day long, now, and the women are all right. The work is just with my hands and my feet and it leaves me with plenty of time to think. Ivy isn't working there now. She missed a few days and then they gave her the sack. But I'm sure she'll get a job somewhere. There are still a few jobs here. She came round Mr Mac's and caused a bit of bother last night. I'll maybe have to look for another place. It sounds worse again up home. I hope you get what you want before you have to strike. Would that mean that nobody would get any pay? How would they manage? It's hard enough for them to manage with the pay they do get.

From your sister
Lizza

She licked the envelope and pressed it down, thinking how far she had come to write a letter on a 'good Sunday' without thinking about it. Mr Mac was civil enough when she popped her head round his door to say goodbye and she skipped off down to the tram stop with a lighter heart. It was a cold invigorating day and she enjoyed the walk.

The wind seemed colder as she got off the second tram for the long walk to the Bamburghs', and she had only taken ten steps when it started to rain. She quickened her steps as her dress and coat started to whip against her legs. A plop on her face was followed by a sharp cut. Hailstones were crashing to the pavement around her. She started to run but was soon drenched, and almost bruised by the hailstones.

By the time she arrived at the Bamburghs' she was wet through, her dress plastered against her legs, her hair in snaky coils underneath her new round hat. The door opened before she knocked, and Dora grabbed her and dragged her in. She was grinning all over her face at Lizza's drowned rat appearance, and Lizza herself started to laugh helplessly when she saw herself in the hall mirror.

They were clutching each other in a friendly fashion
when Mrs Bamburgh appeared, looking flustered, with
Iris behind her.

'Dear me, dear me!'

Dora rather guiltily dropped Lizza's arm and Lizza
tried to peel off her thick coat. As she did so, she caught
sight of Iris's face as she lurked behind her mother. The
girl was smiling, her face lifted to Lizza's. Even in the
turmoil in the hall, Lizza thought that she had never seen
Iris smile directly before. Sometimes she would smile into
space, as though she has some secret of her own. Now here
she was sharing Lizza's laughing despair at her 'drowned
rat' state.

'Take her up to Iris's room, Dora. I'll have to find you
something to wear, Elizabeth. You can't stay in those wet
clothes.' Mrs Bamburgh bustled on ahead and Iris pat-
tered on behind them.

The fire was burning in Iris's bedroom and Dora put
more coal on it from the copper bucket on the green tiled
hearth.

'Take those things off,' she ordered, opening a built-in
cupboard and taking out two pale green towels. Lizza
stood rather awkwardly. 'Get'm off, nobody bothers here,
you know.' Iris was sitting on the bed playing with the
fringe on the cover, as though she was in the room on her
own. Lizza took a breath and stripped off to her vest and
pants. Even they were wet but she was not taking them off.
She had never been this naked in front of other people, not
even her sisters. In her crowded home a complicated
ritual was always observed, so that everybody's modesty
could be preserved.

Dora started to laugh. ''S'no good leaving them on, girl,
you'll get just as chilled.' Lizza stood. 'Here.' She unfurled
a huge towel and draped it front to back over Lizza.
Somehow, Lizza wriggled out of her remaining clothes

and remained wrapped in the towel. Mrs Bamburgh came in with a dark red dressing-gown over her arm.

'Here. Put this on while Dora dries your things.' Dora piled up the clothes and nodded at Lizza as she put it on. Mrs Bamburgh pulled a chair up beside the cosy fire.

'Sit here and dry out and I'll find you something to drink.'

There was a low table beside the fire with children's books on top. Lizza took one and as the flames crackled up she turned the pages, looking at the nursery pictures, enjoying the colours and the charming images. There was a rustle and a thump and Iris was standing just behind her right elbow.

Lizza made a space on the chair and Iris sat in beside her. She started to read the story to Iris as though she were a much smaller child. When Lizza finished that one, Iris picked another book and pushed it on to Lizza's lap, without looking at her and without saying anything to her. They were on to the fourth book when Lizza realised that Mrs Bamburgh was standing very still in the doorway, a tray in her hand, her face flushed with pleasure at what she saw.

'Elizabeth, I've never seen Iris go to anyone like she goes to you. It's just so hard to believe.'

The three of them settled down to have tea and cakes and biscuits in front of the bedroom fire, spending most of the afternoon in desultory conversation. Mrs Bamburgh asked Lizza about her family and her job, and told her about the job she had had in a gown shop before she met Mr Bamburgh. Iris played with the biscuits on plates, putting them into piles and tipping them off on to the tray. Lizza thought if Johnnie had done that, her mother would have been angry. Playing with food was both wasteful and rude. Mrs Bamburgh seemed not to notice. At five there was a knock on the door and Mr Bamburgh, after greeting

Lizza, told his wife that he would walk round to the Smithsons' to collect the twins who were out to tea.

When he had gone Dora came with a pile of clothes over her arm, neatly pressed. They did another modest dance with the two towels and Lizza dressed herself. She stayed standing.

'I've really got to go now. I promised Mr Mac I'd be back at six.'

Mrs Bamburgh stood up with unusual decision. 'I'll walk with you to the tram stop, Elizabeth.' She turned to Dora who was still hovering, draped in towels and the dressing-gown. 'You keep your eye on Iris, Dora. Mr Bamburgh should be back any moment with the boys.'

'Righto.'

'Dora.' The tone was pained. 'How many times do I have to tell you not to say that!'

'Sorry'm.' Dora hung her head but she winked at Lizza with the eye on Mrs Bamburgh's blind side. Lizza gulped back a laugh and thought painfully of her dear Renee, who would have done just that.

It was bitterly cold outside, and Mrs Bamburgh slipped her arm through Lizza's as they walked together down the roads leading to the tram stop. As they walked she talked in a very determined manner about Iris.

'She really was a lovely baby you know. Lovely. She smiled at you when she was only weeks old. Recognised a whole lot of people. Then I had the twins. I had a bad time. The house was like a hospital for a month. Nurses, doctors, rushing backward and forward. When I finally got up, Iris was a changed girl. She just hid in corners and would barely eat anything. She stopped talking and seemed kind of afraid of everyone. It was months before I could get her to go out of the house.'

'She's much better now, then?'

'I suppose so. It's just been such a long time. What I

have noticed though, is the way she comes to you. She's never done that to anyone outside the family.'

Lizza was embarrassed at the flattery that was building up, and still rather awkward with this woman's arm through hers.

'The thing is, Elizabeth, I wondered if you might take up some teaching to Iris? It seems to me that you're a born teacher.'

'Teacher?'

'Anything. Anything you could do with her would be a benefit.'

'Well, Mrs Bamburgh, I've got a job, you know.'

'I know that, but what about Sundays? Could you come every Sunday and do something with her – anything?'

They were at the tram stop. Lizza's head was whirling. She was interested in Iris, but unsure of the tie that this would make. At the back of her mind was the thought that this was just another version of Dora. She would be useful to them, of service.

'Well,' she said, doubtfully, 'I'd mebbe try a few times. Can't think of what I might do.'

Mrs Bamburgh's pale face was urgent. 'You'll think of something, Elizabeth. I know you will.' The tram clanked to a halt in front of them. 'So you'll come next Sunday, at least?'

'Well, yes. Yes. Thank you.'

As she slid into the slatted seat and turned to wave at Mrs Bamburgh she wondered briefly why it should be her, Lizza, who was doing the thanking. Of all the people in that house the one she really liked was Dora, and the more she went to the house as a guest, the more Mrs Bamburgh linked her arm in Lizza's, the greater the distance between Lizza and Dora.

When she got back to the house Mr Mac's light was off, but she could hear him coughing. She wished, briefly, he would see a doctor about that cough. He could afford it. In her room, her coal fire was neatly banked up, so she knew he had been up here, and thinking about her. She climbed into bed, comparatively happily, and slept as soon as her head touched the pillow.

The following Thursday Lizza got two letters, one in her mother's immaculate looping script with little punctuation, the other in the fat sparrow hand of Bea.

Dear Elizabeth,

Bernard has told me all your news it sounds as though you are working hard and doing quite well. What has happened to Ivy you must be careful living there on your own keep yourself to yourself I don't think you should work on a Sunday even if as Bernard says it is good work remember on the seventh day you shall rest it is a rule that gives order to a hard life and grants to the Lord that which is his own life goes on as always here you would hear about poor Mrs Donahue. The children have gone to the Home and Mr Donahue has been acting very strange I have prayed for those children that have lost their mammy and have no hearth of their own. She is in a better place but they have the vale of tears to endure.

Your loving Mother

Dear Lizza,

I can't write anything like as long a letter as you can but I thought you would like to hear from me. You sound as though you have made some friends who will look out for you. I am really pleased about that as Renee and I have thought about you every night as we miss you very much. I had an idea you would make your way, you've got it in you like none of the rest of us have, even Bernard. Life here goes on very much as usual. I have a young man now. He is very handsome with curly blond hair and works in a shop. He walks me and Renee home after work every night and we go dancing twice a week and he is a lovely dancer. One or two lads are interested in our Renee but she had no time for lads. Wants to stay a bairn for ever. Bernard's looking very worried these days. There is real trouble brewing over these latest moves on wages and there are more men out of work who stand on the street corners, or crouch on their hunkers talking the whole day away. I can't think when and how it will all end. Our Johnnie has two rabbits which he's keeping in the yard. He scours the green for rabbit food every night. It might keep him out of mischief. Bernard's taking over the allotment of a man who was killed in the pit, earlier this month. It's planted up and Bernard says gloomily we'll need the produce before the year's out. Anyway there is not much more to say except take care of yourself, pet.

Your loving sister,
Bea   X from Renee

P.S. I am now getting keen on the pictures. Our Bernard said he told you that thing about Da being on the pictures and Ma going to see. Well, ever since, she's been sending me down with some cakes. Mr Chilton lets me watch the pictures, free.

B.

As time went on Mr Mac showed little interest in her. He was polite enough, but there were no more cosy teas. She searched his face as they passed on the stairs, but was met with blank disinterest. His face was thinner and whiter, and the fairish hair too long about his ears. She felt he had forgotten her, as a person, until every night after work she opened the door of her room to a blazing, carefully stoked fire.

In the next few weeks, Sundays at the Bamburghs' fell into a routine. Lizza resisted their urging to come for dinner as well as tea, but started arriving at half past two instead of four and spent the extra time with Iris. Mr Mac was leaving her more and more on her own now, and didn't show interest in where she went. She met her own mother's strictures about not working on Sundays by telling Iris stories from the Bible among other books. She walked with Iris along the dusty suburban lanes, speculating about the trees and plants, and making up stories about the people who lived in the houses. Lizza also steadfastly refused the shower of gifts or offers of cash for the work she did with Iris. For work it was.

Dear Bea,
      Thank you for your letter. I am pleased that you found time to write to me. I think about you and Renee a lot. I still use the embroidered bag which you made. Lots of people have said how nice it is and I use it all the time.
      You would be interested in Iris, the girl in the family where I go to on a Sunday afternoon. She's about thirteen and nearly as tall as me, but you would really think she's about eight – no, four. She doesn't talk at all. She hasn't said anything since she was three when her twin brothers were born. Anyway, the Bamburghs have asked me to see if I can teach her anything. And hard work it is. I have got her to sit while I read her stories. I got 'The King of the Golden River' from a second-hand

book shop, and Iris liked that and touched the pictures with her fingers. Can you remember we had it at school? It has those lovely curly black pictures that run right round the print. It has taken ages to get Iris even to look me in the eyes. In the end I held her face in my fingers and laughed at her for so long that she smiled too, and didn't turn her head away. I take her for walks in the roads round here but haven't walked far enough to see any green or any hills.

I sometimes think of the rims of green that you could see even from the narrowest pit streets at home. I do this work with Iris on a Sunday, but I don't take any pay of any kind and (you can tell Ma) I tell her a lot of Bible stories.

I must go now and get to bed. I am so tired.

> Love to Renee and Johnnie and
> Bernard and Mam,
> Lizza

P.S. Fancy you having a young man. I bet a lot of them are fighting over you.
P.P.S. Please tell Bernard I'm waiting for a letter from him.

Dear Mam,
It was lovely to get your letter and I will think of your advice. I hear our Johnnie has some rabbits. That's very nice. He's wanted a rabbit for a long time. I haven't heard from Ivy, but I will let you know as soon as I do.

> Your loving daughter,
> Lizza

The third week in April started pretty normally. There was more to be done at work as Mrs Cobbett was away. Lizza went to see her on the Tuesday night straight after work, finding her way down the narrow and narrower streets till she came to the narrow entry on to which Mrs Cobbett's house opened. Children were tumbling round the entry making the most of the evening light to play. Women were leaning on doorposts waiting for their men to come from work. They watched her with interest but did not speak. She was conscious of the lightness of her shoes on the cobbles and the fact that her hair, washed and dried in front of the fire on Sunday night, was clean. She felt that being clean, here, was giving offence, a kind of boasting.

She knocked on the door and walked in on hearing a voice. She let herself into a dark little room which was quite cold.

'Oh, it's you, Lizza.' The voice coming from the heap on the sofa had its usual cheer but was reedy and thin. She made out Mrs Cobbett's face at the end of a heap of clothes on the sofa and saw that the small fireplace had no fire in it.

'Hello, how are you? You must be very cold in here.'

'Well, lass, I've got all the blankets and coats in the house on me. But it is cold and it's beyond me at the minute to light my fire. My leg seems gone altogether with this cold I've got.'

'Can I light it for you?' She put down her basket and pulled on her apron and set about the task while she gave Mrs Cobbett the news from work, and Mrs Cobbett told her about feeling dizzy with a cold and slipping on her bad leg and it being impossible to put a foot down.

'It'll be all right in a few days. It's happened before – but in the meanwhile I can't get about at all.'

Lizza watched with pleasure as the fire crackled into life

and she heaped the coal on from the bucket on the hearth. She thought how she hated housework when she did it for her mother or for Mrs Martindale. Now, clear of the duty and industry, it was a pleasure to make the room cosy for her friend. She picked up the kettle and looked for a tap. There was no other room, just a curtain which covered the staircase.

'You'll have to go to the end of the entry for the tap.' Mrs Cobbett informed her. 'No kitchen here you know, just the bedroom upstairs and this room. Take the big jug, it'll hold far more than the kettle.'

It was darker outside when Lizza went out with the jug. The women in the doorways were gone but she nearly tripped over two children who still rolled around in the gloom. When she came back with the full jug, Mrs Cobbett had pulled herself into a sitting position on the sofa and was straightening up her higgledy-piggledy covers. She put her hand to her hair, very wispy with days-old braids.

'I'm a real mess.'

'Don't worry about that. We'll have a cup of tea and these iced buns I got at Gibsons. Then I'll do your hair. I don't know that I could get the braids up, though.'

Mrs Cobbett gave a fragile laugh. 'Why, duck, if you get a brush through it, it'll be a relief, and a tidy plait'll do for now.'

Lizza spent a pleasant hour being useful, plaiting Mrs Cobbett's hair, bringing her a dish of water to wash her face, talking about work and the neighbourhood. She set up two chairs beside the couch with a lamp and comb and other things Mrs Cobbett might find useful in the night. Before she went she banked up the fire as well as she could and put a fireguard round it. She was pleased that her friend did not make too much fuss, just lay quietly accepting it all.

It was dark when she got back into the entry, with more light at the far end where it opened into wider streets. She was turning round this corner when she bumped into two men in working clothes, as dirty and black-greased as the entry she had just left.

The taller, heavier one, a man in his mid-thirties, grasped her arm above the elbow.

'What have we got here, Jack? A ginger cat, a little ginger cat.' The smaller man, younger with a narrow face stroked her coat. 'Here, pussy! Here, pussy!'

The big man was pulling her back into the entry. 'Come and see if we can find some cream, Ginger.' She pulled back, thinking how she had hated being called Ginger at school, and later, and retching at the foul working-smell of the men. She pulled back the hand that had her basket in it and smashed it right across both of their heads with a wild sweep. They loosened their hold and she started to run.

'Hey, Ginger, no need for that.' They shouted and followed her down two or three streets, but were not in condition to keep up the chase with someone as fit and well-fed as Lizza.

She ran on, even when she knew they were not following her, her feet rattling on the pavement, her heart pounding and her breath coming in short gasps. She took deep breaths on the doorstep before letting herself in, then quietly made her way up to her own room. At first she had wanted to rush in to Mr Mac to tell him of her experience, but as that idea formed she decided to keep it to herself. She didn't know why except that she felt that somehow she had done something wrong and that she had to deal with it herself. Mr Mac, anyway, wouldn't be interested.

When Lizza called on Mrs Cobbett the next night, the older woman was hobbling about in her day clothes and looking much less fragile. They had tea together and Lizza brushed out her hair and she herself put it up in its customary braids. Lizza found herself telling her what had happened the night before. Mrs Cobbett made a wry mouth. 'More of that round here than is decent. You just have to keep yourself to yourself as far as you can.' She hobbled across to the mantelpiece and brought down two long hatpins with fancy heads, one silver and one pearl. 'One in each hand and you'll do enough damage to get away another time.'

Lizza took them – they were very pretty. The silver one was finely worked. 'I'll give you them back.'

'No. You keep them. They were my mother's from better times.'

They sat together as the light faded, drinking tea and eating the biscuits that Lizza had brought. Taking the opportunity, Lizza asked a question that had teased her for a long time.

'What happened for your leg to get like that?'

'Nearly six years now. I'd been working right from the time my boys went away. On the looms then. Known for a good worker. Singer used to get me to train the new starters. Not that it made any difference to the wages, poor then as they are now. Anyway, there was this girl – new starter – who went kind of crazy. She started to race through the place with this big chock of wood she'd picked up somewhere. Thrashing round at the machines and anyone who got near her. Anyway Singer came for me. He sent all the others away and I started to talk to her. She quietened down a bit and I got near her but as I moved forward I tripped on a rickety board and fell down, almost on to her. Then the rage started again and she started to kick. I pulled my knee up to protect me, but by the time Singer and the others had got to her, her clogs had done a lot of damage.'

'And that made you lame?'

'Well, they got me home and I stayed there a couple of days. Singer came to see me and got me off to hospital. But the damage had been done. There were two breaks and a lot of bruising on the spine. It's never been right since. Couldn't stand for the looms any more, so Singer got me this job. He was very good you know. Paid the doctor's bills or got the boss to pay the doctor's bills. Did well there. Like getting blood out of a stone.'

'That's awful, made lame because you wanted to help somebody.'

'You just have to take these things, Lizza. Wasn't nobody's fault. Not even poor Harriet Lamb's. She ended up in the asylum, so she's been well punished for it, poor soul.'

She glanced at the window. 'Hey, Lizza, it's time you was gone. It's gettin' right dark now.'

Lizza stood up, reluctant to leave the companionable space. 'Are you sure you'll be all right?'

'I'll be fine, Lizza. Don't you worry about me. I'll be back at work before you can say Jack Robinson.' Mrs Cobbett's face, haloed by its pretty braids, was quite tranquil, so, with a hatpin in each hand, Lizza set out for home through the dark alleyways.

Mrs Cobbett managed to hobble to work on Friday, looking grey in the face but very determined. Mr Singer brought her in and sat her at the corner of the table. He looked round at the old women round the table and at Lizza.

'Now, Mavis is to stay here. She's not to walk around. Any walking around, you lot do.' The old women nodded and grumbled and snuffled in agreement. Lizza, standing with her bobbin basket, looked from the colour-drained, stressed face of her friend to that of Mr Singer showing uncharacteristic concern. He bustled away without saying anything further. Mrs Cobbett managed to work quite well from her chair, asking Lizza and the women when she needed anything.

At two in the afternoon Mr Singer reappeared. His face, so recently benevolent and concerned with regard to Mavis Cobbett, was black and angry.

'Lizza. In my office, if you please.'

'What's up, Mr Singer?'

'I asked you to go to my office.' He stalked off.

She put down her basket and looked at Mrs Cobbett. 'You'd better go, love. No holding him when he's like that.'

She trailed through the mill with a dull, lumpy feeling inside, furiously and fruitlessly trying to think of what she had done wrong.

He was sitting behind his desk in his cluttered office. He pushed a brown envelope at her.

'What is it?'

'It's your pay and your notice.'

'Notice? What've I done? I thought I was working all right. All the women said so.'

'It's not what you've done. It's who you are, or more accurately, who you're related to.'

'Related to?' She felt uncharacteristically stupid.

'Your sister came – '

'Ivy? I haven't seen her for weeks.'

' – your sister came and told me she'd come to get your wages.'

'Wages? She doesn't get my wages. Not now.'

'Well, today she thinks she does. Came here demanding them as though she had a right.' His face went red. 'She was drunk and – er – abusive. She used some terrible language regarding – er – my character. She threw things.'

Lizza felt near to laughing, or crying.

'But Mr Singer, that's not my fault.'

'May be not your fault, but it's a consequence of your being here. It's happened once and can happen again. I am not prepared to – er – permit that.' His voice was strong and his manner very resolved. There would be no moving him. She was silent.

'So your pay here includes today, so I'd be grateful if you would finish your shift.'

She picked up the envelope and folded her lips together to stop any tears.

'Well, I'm sorry you've been embarrassed, Mr Singer. It's been good working here. People have been very kind.'

She turned round and pushed her way through his door. The noise of the mill invaded her as she walked through, taking all her thoughts from her and making her brain numb. She banged the door of the bobbin shed, and leaned against it.

'What's up?' Mavis Cobbett was looking over with concern, her hands stilled over the bobbins.

'Given the sack. Our Ivy came to try and get my wages. Shouted at him and threw things, he said. Just work out today.' She picked up the basket. The old women's fingers were busy, their eyes were kind.

'What'll you do?' Old Joan had picked up the significance.

'Don't know. Look for another job.' She started to collect the bobbins. They and her feet were heavy, her shoulders sagged. She reached over for Mrs Cobbett's finished bobbins. The older woman took her wrist. 'Why not go home? You must have some money saved now.'

'Yes, I've got some money. But there's no jobs there, even if I go.'

'You don't have to stay. Just go back and see your mother and your family. It's hard on you, this.'

'I might do that.'

Lizza felt the sullen and weighty doubt inside her. Bernard would be pleased to see her. Renee and Bea would be pleased as well. Johnnie might just distract himself from his rabbits to play a friendly trick on her. She could see all the hugs and smiles, hear the delighted words of welcome. But all her mind's eye would produce of her mother was the powerful image of her standing straight in the doorway of the pit house, looking hard, almost accusingly, and she heard again the words, 'Different, you are.'

She heaved the basket on to her hip and looked down at Mrs Cobbett.

'Maybe you're right. I will go home.'

'You do that. And, mind you, when you come back, be sure to come and see me. You've been good . . .' Mrs Cobbett's eyes went back on to the bobbin at her fingers. 'Mebbe you could write to me. I haven't had a letter in a lot of years. Not since the war, if you don't count Reuben.'

12 Catastrophe

The house smelt cold as she opened the big door. She tried Mr Mac's sitting-room door. It was locked. She felt heavy, like a stone. He was never out, he had to be sitting here, just not wanting to see her. There was no one to tell, to tell what had happened today, to share the crisis.

There was a letter on the hall stand in Bernard's graceful hand. She picked it up and wearily made her way upstairs. Her fire, unusually, was unlit; the air in the room was raw, unwarmed. Unusually also, last night's ashes were still in the firegrate. Mr Mac's anger and dislike was seeping into her own space, into her own body. She flopped down on to the bed to read the letter, her eyes stubbornly dry.

Dear Lizza,

I hope you're all right. Sometimes I think your letters say a lot and at the same time nothing at all. You do know don't you, that if things aren't so good you can always come home. We'll manage somehow. Even so that needs to be a last resort. But you do know that the work situation here is impossible and with the strike looming up things will likely get much worse. But remember your home is here. Maybe I shouldn't say it but the less you see of our Ivy, the better. I wish I could get down to see you but it's not possible as things are now. Sundays are filled with planning meetings so I can't even come on a weekend.

Ma is pleased you are doing well. She lets people know – in her own way – that you've got a good job.

Anyway, write soon and tell me how things are with you. How things really are. It will be all right, Ma doesn't read your letters, I just read bits out to her.

Love,
Bernard

She sat down and smoothed the creases out of the letter on the lumpy quilt. That was it then. She would go home, maybe not for long. A short time. The saved money would pay her way. She wouldn't be a burden on them. She pursed her lips and rejected the self-pitying tears. What had she to do? She had to pack. She had to let the Bamburghs know so Iris wouldn't look for her.

She moved around the room in a trance, taking out clothes, shaking them and folding them very carefully. The new shoes were wrapped in newspaper. Mr Mac's gifts, books and ornaments she left in an orderly group on the mantelpiece. She cleared the fire out, taking the ashes downstairs and out to the yard. Mr Mac's door remained stubbornly shut as she walked noisily past.

She was very cold when she arrived at the Bamburghs' house. Dora's face was a picture of concern when she saw her.

'What's up. Is there something wrong?'

'What is it, Dora?' Mrs Bamburgh was not far behind her, concerned about a late caller.

She was hustled into the parlour where Mr Bamburgh was just buttoning up his jacket. He listened carefully to her story and glanced over at his wife.

'Well, I think you are right to go home and see your people. What is it, two months since we travelled down together?'

Mrs Bamburgh interrupted, 'But you must come back.'

Lizza turned to Iris, 'I won't be here for a little while,

Iris, so I thought I'd come and tell you.' Iris looked dumbly at her, her eyes watching Lizza with a pleasing curiosity. Lizza was at a loss to know what to do. She fished in the embroidered bag and found the brooch that Bernard had given her. She leaned over and pinned it on to Iris's ruffled nightdress.

'I'm going away, Iris, and I want you to take care of my brooch for me.' Iris smiled at her. Lizza left the room and followed Mrs Bamburgh downstairs. Mr Bamburgh was talking to Dora in the back hall.

Mrs Bamburgh held her by the elbow and put her cheek against Lizza's. 'Goodbye, my dear girl. Do come back to us.'

Mr Bamburgh had sent Dora into the night to run for a taxi, and Lizza was soon bundled in. As she peered out of the taxi window she could see the troubled face of Dora, the tearful face of Mrs Bamburgh, the stern face of Mr Bamburgh, and the white smudges of the faces of the twins in the bay window.

Lizza was trembling from head to foot all the way back. Whether it was excitement or exhaustion or the return of her childhood disease she didn't know. Whatever it was she felt aware of things, as though, despite the speed, they were travelling through the town in an enormous exaggerated slowness. It seemed that even a blink of her eye took a full minute and as she alighted from the taxi each separate movement took a full five minutes.

Her shoes clicked as she walked across the black and white tiled floor, and she averted her gaze from Mr Mac's door, not wanting again to see the rejecting closure.

Then, without her brain willing it, she turned round again, approached the closed door, and knocked hard. Her knock resounded as though through a room empty of people, only singing off hard surfaces. She tried the handle. The door seemed locked. Then again, without her brain willing it, she gave a hard shove. The door gave, just a little. There was something jammed up against it. She pushed harder and made a narrow space through which she squeezed with considerable difficulty.

The room was in darkness but the curtains were undrawn and the town glow seeped into the unlit space. There was a cold draught from the sash window which was wide open.

She felt at her feet for whatever was blocking the door. Her hand touched hair and cold flesh which might have been burning hot for the speed with which her hand recoiled. She looked down. The borrowed light from the window fixed on the long fairish hair, turning it to gold.

She stumbled across to his little kitchen and lit his lamp with the matches that were always on the pantry shelf. Coming back into the cluttered room the lines of light from the lantern picked up the table and the bookcases that she loved. She walked unsteadily to the lumpish thing that had stopped the door opening. The warm yellow light illuminated bluish flesh and wide open eyes, the golden fair hair was stiff as though it were cut out of cardboard. Mr Mac was dead, quite as dead as any of Johnnie's rabbits. One side of her mind told her you would always know, really, when anyone was dead. She tried to reach to close the eyes but she couldn't. She swallowed very hard, then went to put the lamp on the table and squeezed back out of the room.

She really needed to go home now. 'Mammy, why did you let me come here to this place? I have to come home now.' She spoke the words out loud through lips made of cork, soft but stiff. She pushed the door open to make sure one of the other lodgers passing would see the light and call in, and with leaden feet, went up for her case, her coat and her bag.

The long train journey home was silent. Despite kindly overtures she remained numbly uncommunicative. The whole of her inside ached with a pain that was partly hunger, as she had not eaten since Friday breakfast, before she had got the sack from work. As well as this there was a kind of tension inside her that made her feel sick all the time. She had walked the Bradford streets for some hours, trailing her bags with her, then finally slithered down a muddy slope and crouched there under a canal bridge for most of the night. In those hours she had worked out that it must be Gil again, back for money on a Friday, or even Ivy. They had hurt him somehow and he had fallen by the door and they had got out of the window.

The train lurched and rattled. The loaf-like face of Constable Mogdan kept coming in front of her. She had run away. He would blame her, she felt sure. She was stiff after her night under the bridge, but had dusted off the worst of the dirt before catching a workmen's tram to the railway station. At the station she had managed to take her hair down and comb it with the comb that had been Bea's present. She had spat on her hankie and cleaned her face, and looked round anxiously for pursuing policemen sent by the assiduous Constable Mogdan. There had been a policeman, but he was collecting something – a parcel – from the Station Master's office. He went off through the great arched doorway, whistling.

She finally drifted away into a troubled and uncomfortable sleep, lulled, despite her worries, by the rhythmic click of the carriage working its way along a thousand rails.

'Dur-ham! Dur-ham!'

Durham! She jumped up and gathered her bags, and was off the train almost before she was awake. The pleasure at being so near home, for just one moment,

blotted out the harassing circumstances that had brought
her here. She stood alone among the cases and the bustling travellers, looking round. She ached for the miracle of
a familiar face, but the faces that looked back at her were
friendly enough, but all strange.

Lizza finally stood alone in the station above the town,
wondering how to get home. Durham was only four miles
distant from her home village but she had never, till this
moment, been there, in the town. She looked across at the
looming bulk of the castle, the delicate tracery of the
cathedral. Gold stone counterpointed with the grey in the
afternoon sun. Down below she could see the steep streets
and the narrow houses and the glitter of the river.

'Standing wondering, love?' a uniformed man stacking
parcels into the parcel bay shouted over.

'I need to get a bus to Brack Hill. Is there a bus?'

'Just go down to the bottom of the hill, love. Can't miss
it.' His face was thin, his eyes narrow and searching. Then
he smiled and she could see him at home with his children,
anxious but always loving.

She smiled back. 'Thank you.' It was hard to smile.

''S'all right, bonny lass.' His eyes left her face, moving
to the mass of her hair. He turned back to his stacking. She
turned back to the town and set off down the hill, changing
her heavy case, from time to time, from weary arm to
weary arm. She began to regret the impulse that had
urged her to stuff the case full of almost random items, to
make sure she went home with full, not empty, hands.

As she walked, the mass of masonry linking the castle
and the cathedral seemed to flatten, and loom nearer to
her. As she walked down the hill she kept her eyes on them
till at last they were masked by the height of the buildings
at ground level.

There were several bus stops, and a bus which the
driver said was going to Chester-le-Street. A bus in her

direction in another hour and a half. She plumped the case down, wearily.

'Come far, have you?' It was an old man, sitting on his haunches against the wall beside the bus stop. He had a dark scarf round his stringy neck and a coat fastened by rope at the waist. The face was small, eyes round, nose tip-tilted giving an impossibly youthful look.

'Yes. From Bradford.'

'Long way that. On Bradford station a whole night I was, once. In the war.'

She nodded without speaking, trying to stop him with her mind. In her mind, imprinted, was the rising mass of the cathedral, set by with a castle, an amazing castle, framed in the window of the railway carriage and veiled in the steam and the dropping soot of the train as it slowed down in the station. She had seen it on the way to Bradford. She saw it on her way back. She picked up her heavy case.

'You off, then?' His surface-merry face grimaced up at her.

She nodded and started to walk along the wide street towards the cathedral. The buildings on either side were tall, reminiscent of some parts of Bradford. There were some shops with people drifting in and out, but the town was quiet. She came to a bridge over the broad river. The steeply-rising river banks were spikily clad in reaching branches of the spring trees, ready to explode with green. High above them, first the warm yellow stone of the castle with its battlements, then the grey strength of the stone of the cathedral. She shifted her heavy case to the other hand, relishing the temporary release from pain.

She climbed down to a patch which led the way along the side of the river, she changed the case to the other hand, then looked down at it. There were dense bushes leaning against the wall of the stone steps. She pulled them out, thrust the case in and pulled the bushes back, glancing round as she did so. There were people walking slowly above, on the bridge, all with their heads up, about their own business. She set off, picking up a twig from a bush to swish as she walked.

Within five minutes she was at a crossing place, a broad handsome bridge with standing places inset at intervals along, so you could see over the wall up to the battlements or along the river. A voice spoke. She jumped.

'That's quite something, don't you think?'

She looked swiftly at the person who had spoken and returned her gaze to the mass of masonry opposite. She nodded slowly, allowing the edge of her eye to survey the boy, then turned her back on him. A young man, with a heavy coat and a tweed cap pulled to one side. He was taller and heavier than her – at least a year older – white hair cut short over the ears, pale eyes with shadows underneath. She felt, she knew, she had seen him before. Where?

13 *Lizza meets Roland King*

The week before he actually met Lizza on the river-bank
Roland King had written to his father.

Dear Father,
   I write though I have not heard from you. I
imagine you have spent many weeks afloat and this
might reach you at your next port. I wonder if it might
be Patagonia? I had occasion recently to meet Mr
Silkin, the Bishop Auckland lawyer. He is a kind and
generous man, I think, and mentioned his wife's kind
thoughts about Mama.
   Since last writing I have actually met and talked to a
miner working here in the coalfield. We met on a bus.
He seemed a very gentle person and talked very elo-
quently about his concerns in the present situation. He
made a good deal of sense and did not seem in the least
the monstrous Bolshevik painted by our teachers. Is
that why the Bolsheviks are so dangerous, that somehow they seem so sensible? Meeting this miner made
me think that we are a rock of ignorance at school, in a
sea of knowledge. Rather than the reverse, as the
teachers would have it. Having said that I will now get
the maid to post this.

                    Your loving son,
                    Roland

Now Roland stood stiffly erect beside the monitor's
door.

'King!' The high-pitched voice exploded from within. 'I, with my magnificent brain, can perceive in your tiny mind the desire to move, the desire to move your foot, to move your arm, to twitch that ungainly nose. Am I not right?' The voice demanded agreement.

'Yes, Foxer.'

'And what happens if such extremities so much as tremble?'

'Another week, Foxer.'

'Another week. Just standing out there, every minute of your spares. Just think, King.'

'Yes, Foxer.' He swayed to his left, trying to ease the numbness of his right leg. The halo of lights on the outside edges of his eyes started to shimmer in on him again. The invading lights had attacked him increasingly during his two-hour forced vigil. He could hear Foxer's voice again but it was pleasingly distant. He swayed to his left side to ease the numbness in his left leg, then fell, cracking his head on the heavy oak of the door frame. His blood smeared the very paint at the corner and was flowing from the swelling cut a second later when Foxer, a tall thin boy with his face oddly drawn to the centre, opened the door.

'King. Oh Lord!' Foxer leaned over and pulled him in. There'd be trouble here. Better clean the kid up and bring him round. He pulled him on to one of the two high beds in the narrow room. Roland could see through laden eyes the sports vest that Foxer was using to mop up the blood. It flooded on to his hand and he swore a favourite and forbidden word. A bell rang, a distant echo transmitted through the stone corridors. Foxer shook Roland, who let his head roll. 'Damn you, King.' Foxer flung him down again, picked up some books and went out of the room, slamming the door.

Roland sat up, swung his legs round and sat in front of the fire on a chair, rubbing his numb legs and wincing at

the sharp pain in his head. He found the bloodstained vest
and, spitting on a corner of it, carefully cleaned the blood
off his face, leaving the slight clot that was stopping the
flow. He peered through the window at the figures scuttling across the road to the main building. In a few
minutes the outside walkways were empty. The boys had
scurried to their holes like rabbits to a warren.

He left the room, past the site of his recent torture, and
went down the staircase. On the pegs inside the main door
was an old tweed coat. On his many weary journeys to and
from Foxer's room, he had noticed it hanging there,
unclaimed, for several months. It was not a uniform coat.
It was probably some holiday coat of an old boy or visitor,
left and neglected, waiting for his need, now. He scooped
it up and slowly walked down the drive of the house, out
into the lane, with the coat under his arm. When he got to
the woods above the river, he pulled it on and belted it
lightly. Putting his hand inside the pocket he found a
tweed cap, folded into itself. He pulled this down on to his
head, well down over the injured right eye.

Then he started to make his way down through the trees
to the river. The dead straw of last year's growth crackled
under his feet but the spring bulbs and new grass were
showing under the trees. Only the well-worn paths pre-
vented growth and showed the old ways down on to the
river-bank.

He could see the broad glimmer of the river between the
trees and looking up could see his beloved cathedral.
There, he would go there first. Then he would set out for
John Silkin's. He had no money so he would have to walk.
There was a flash of red in the shrubs by the bank. He
stood still, thinking he would see a squirrel, as he had
many times before.

It was a girl's head, showing only the back of her hair,
as she made her way along the bank with her face always

to the cathedral. She wore a dark green coat and her bushy hair was tied back at the nape of her neck and looped up somehow. It was shining like a chestnut from a newly split shell.

Quietly, slowly, he made his way down the bank, slithering sometimes but always silent, towards Lizza who was standing by the bridge, then spoke to her.

She turned to look at him and was met by grey eyes, under-marked by shadow. She turned back, turning her body entirely to get him out of even her peripheral vision.

A hand grasped her elbow and she wrenched away and started to walk quickly across the bridge, finding herself on a narrow path which ran alongside the high cathedral wall. Footsteps crunched behind her. She came to a dead end. To one side was a high arched doorway which led up a narrow tunnel, an arch of light in the distance indicating its length.

'I say!' The soft-toned voice was breathless. 'Steady on! I just want to talk to you.'

She stood still in the shadow of a buttress. 'What is it you want to talk about, then?'

'About . . . me.'

'What about you?'

'I've had the most awful day and your hair was so bright against the grey stone, so I had to speak to you.'

She relaxed. It was all harmless enough and an indication of genuine interest. Just ask a question back:

'Why's it been such a bad day?'

'Well, Foxer, he's the monitor . . .'

'Monitor?'

'Yes. At school. My school's at the top of this bank here.'

'We had monitors at school. I was one once, when I was in the top class.'

'Were you?' He looked surprised. 'You don't look old enough.' She said nothing.

'Anyway, Foxer's had me standing to attention outside his study for two hours today, and all my spare time this week.'

'Today? What are you doing at school today? It's SATURDAY!'

'I'm at school every day. I'm there all the time.'

'You sleep there?'

'Yes.'

'Don't you miss your ma and da then? And your brothers and sisters?'

He leaned up against the stone wall and looked back across the river to the path she had walked along. A man and a small girl were walking along it now, hand in hand. 'Well, you see my mother's dead and my father's at sea, and I've no brothers and sisters. So home or away, they wouldn't miss me.'

She was looking at him with interest now. 'So you live at school? I sometimes used to think I'd like that, when I was at school. To be there all the time and read all the books in peace and quiet.' Just for a second the golden hair and the dead eyes were forgotten.

'You liked school then?'

'Oh yes. I loved it. Wanted it to go on for all time. Don't you, then?'

'There are some parts of it I like. But not being shut in so much. Do you know four of my great-grandfathers were at sea? When you've got the sea in your blood you don't like to be shut in. Then there are people like Foxer. They can make things very difficult.'

'What did you do to make him do that to you?'

'Well, he likes people to call him sir. So one day I didn't and he warned me. The next day I called him Sir Archie. So he gave me a week's waits.'

'Waits?'

'Waiting outside his door in all my spare time.'

'Sounds silly to me.'

'It's not so bad. Worse things happen.' He moved closer to her in the shadow of the buttress, and she flinched back, but he put his finger to his lips to stop her calling out.

Two men in almost identical tweed suits were moving up the path deep in conversation. They may have glanced at the young couple talking in the shadows, but the tweed cap and coat was an effective disguise.

Roland waited until they had turned into the tunnel archway before he spoke.

'Teachers,' he hissed, '. . . 'Ganton and Flood. Didn't spot me.' He pulled off his cap to shake his startling white hair back and she noticed the bloody cut just above the right eye.

'That looks bad.'

'Just a wound in the ongoing battle with Fateful Foxer.'

The lighthearted words belied the heavy feeling in his stomach. He was heartily sick of Foxer's two-term campaign and wondered how long he could hold out. No. Now he wouldn't need to. He wondered what John Silkin would say when he turned up on his doorstep.

He jammed the cap back on to his head.

'Anyway, I'm going up to touch the knocker, then I'm going on to see a friend of my father's. He's a lawyer in a town about eight miles from here.'

'What do you mean, touch the knocker?'

'In the old days anyone, even a murderer, was safe from pursuit once he'd touched the knocker.'

'I wouldn't mind seeing that.'

'Come on then. Everyone needs to be safe from pursuit sometimes.' He took her arm and this time she didn't pull away. Then he led her up the narrow arched passageway and out into an old square. Three sides of the square were occupied with tall houses with large square-paned windows. The fourth side was the cathedral.

'This is the back end of the cathedral. To get to the great door we have to get right round the other side.' He led her through a large archway up one street, then up a narrow cobbled lane.

They were standing on a small patch of green with the strangely diminished bulk of the castle on their right and the gracious rise of the cathedral on their left, its arching window pointing a blunt finger to the sky, its ancient greying bulk in great shadows on the right. As they walked together on the path towards the door, Lizza felt hot in the wool coat and rather hemmed in by the hand still clasping her elbow.

They were dwarfed by the door, but there, within reach, was the leering gargoyle face, covered with the faintly blue sour bloom of old brass, looking wisely and cunningly down. Roland reached up his hand and clasped the heavy ring dropping from the gargoyle's mouth. Using his other hand, he brought up her hand, and laid it on the knocker, beside his.

'There. We are both safe from pursuit. Though we may have done murder we'll survive with our lives.'

She shivered as he declaimed the words in a melodramatic fashion in his clipped voice. Had she done murder? Was it her actions, her presence that had finally led to Mr Mac being slumped against the door?

'I don't know your name.'

'Roland. And yours?'

'Lizza. Short for Elizabeth.'

'Well, Lizza, we are safe now. Safe from pursuit.'

'Will you be pursued?'

'I imagine so, when they find I am gone. Which may be some time. Last time I got out and back in in three hours. This time I'm going for good, though.'

'Won't your father send you back?'

'With being at sea he doesn't really have a say. It's my guardian, Uncle Harry, who has the say. He doesn't want me, so he'll shuttle me back. So, after I've seen Silkin, that's my father's lawyer, I'm walking to Newcastle to see if I can get on a ship. They take you as a deckhand.'

'Running away to sea! That's just a story-book thing.' There was sneering disbelief in her voice.

'I assure you that it is done.' He was offended, his voice became more clipped, his tone pompous.

'Don't be like that. Mebbe it does happen outside story-books. I don't know anything about the navy.' She changed the subject. 'Anyway I'm really hungry. Can we find a place for a cup of tea?' They should go; not be in one place too long.

'There are places. But I can't go. I have no money.'

'Don't worry. I have some. Will your disguise hold up for us to go into the town?'

'I can't let a girl buy me tea, it's not on.'

'What if I was your sister?'

'Well . . .'

'That's all right then, I'm your sister.' They were still holding the knocker.

'My sister.' He smiled broadly, then burst into laughter. She joined in, not sure whether she was laughing at the ridiculousness of the idea, or the fun of the exercise. Her heart eased with the laughing, as though a hand had stopped clenching it.

The small door inset in the large door creaked open and the narrow ravaged face of an old man peered out. His long black surplice had the effect of making his head float in air.

'Do you want something?' The voice was gentle, like Roland's. 'You may come in if you wish.'

'Thank you, we are all right.' Lizza spoke politely.

Roland had turned his head away, and was walking down the path. She ran to catch up.

'He knows me, I didn't want him to see me. We go up to the abbey every week.'

In a few minutes they were into the narrow windy streets of the town.

'Here,' said Lizza. 'This looks like a place.'

She could make out 'Thurstan's Tea Rooms' in green lettering edged with gold. There were red curtains at the windows and she could see white clothed tables. It reminded her of Swinburn's in Bradford. She remembered her tentative feeling as she had been ushered in by Mrs Bamburgh. She opened the door purposefully. It was a small place. Only ten tables, three of which were occupied.

'In the corner,' Roland whispered fiercely, and she led the way to a corner table which was half screened from the room by a flourishing plant on a stand. Roland sat with his back to the room.

The waitress, a heavy old lady with hair in plaits coiled round her ears, came for their order, and Lizza asked for a pot of tea and some teacakes. The old lady looked down at Roland.

'We like the gentlemen to take off their hats in here, if you don't mind.' A thick voice, but proper.

There was a frozen silence. Roland signalled to Lizza with wide grey eyes. His blond, ball-cotton hair would be a sure give-away. Lizza coughed and laughed at the same time. She remembered now where she had seen him.

'We are aware of that, of course.' Her accent mimicked the more correct intonation of Mrs Bamburgh. 'The problem is, my brother is just out of hospital with a head injury. The doctor advises me that he must keep his hat on for another week.'

Red patches stained the old woman's cheeks and she smiled thinly.

'Well, in that case, I think it will be all right.' She clipped her pencil into her book and stalked off.

'Well done! Well done!' Roland was grinning broadly. Lizza reverted to her own speech. 'I don't like being told what to do.'

'Where did you learn to talk like that?'

''S'easy enough. I'm friendly with these people in Bradford. They used their 'ings' and their 'haitches', like you. But not quite. Where d'you come from? You sound like a doctor or a vicar.'

'Ely. When we still had a house. It's in the south. It has a cathedral too, you would like it.'

'Would I?'

The old lady came bustling back with a tray, putting out china cups and silver teapot and jugs, and a silver container with the teacakes. She finally flounced off, and Lizza set about pouring tea.

'What about you? Are you a member of a family?'

She smiled across her hands, holding the teapot with both of them as she carefully poured out his tea.

'Oh yes. There's my mother. My da is dead. He was killed in the last weeks of the war.'

'I'm sorry.'

'Well it was a long time ago now. Eight years. He was there right from the beginning. He was wounded once, and came home twice, and got the Military Medal.'

'He must have been a brave man.'

'That's what his officer said when he came to see my mother, after the war.'

He put sugar in his tea and cut his teacake with the heavy silver knife. It reminded him of before, at home, when his mother was still alive.

He took a mouthful of cake, jam running down his chin, and spoke to her:

'Do you know Durham pretty well, then?'

'No.'

'Don't you live here, then?'

'No. I live in Bradford now. I really came from a place near here, though.' She was conscious of the raw sound of her voice against his.

'You'll have been in Durham before, then?' The gentle tone of his voice pierced her again.

'No. Never. I'm only in this town today off the train.'

'Why did you come here?'

She didn't really know why. To get away from the poor dead body of Mr Mac? To get away from Gil and Ivy, and from the menacing pursuit of Constable Mogdan? But why here, wandering round the flat reaches of a river, loomed over by a castle and a cathedral nudging each other for a space in the sky? Why home anyway when they didn't want her? That's what Bernard's letter had really said. Maybe she needed to feel safe, to be able to take for granted everyone around her, be surrounded by people whose faces, whose very fingernails were as familiar to her as her own.

''Cos I wanted to.'

He could see her discomfort. He changed the subject.

'What about brothers and sisters?'

'Two brothers and three sisters.'

'Are they all away from home?'

'No. Only my oldest sister and me. The rest are still at home.' He saw the corner of her lip crease, making her whole face look cross.

'Do you mind being away?'

'I did at first. It was so different. You were so much on

your own. I think I'm used to it now. I like being responsible for myself.'

'Which one's your favourite?'

'Well, I like them all, see. But really it's Bernard who I'm close too, and Renee. Bernard's the oldest, and was a good scholar and we talk about books. And Renee, well she's kind and she's funny. Sometimes she's quite rude, but . . .' She coloured. She had been almost talking to herself and then caught sight of his intense look and been embarrassed.

'They sound interesting. I wish I had a brother and sister.'

'They're all right. You can come and meet them if you like.' It was a joke, but looking at the pale eyes in the pale face, she knew that she did want him to come with her. Take the heat off her walking in unannounced, loaded with trouble.

'I'm going to John Silkin's. That lawyer fellow.'

'Where does he live?'

'Bishop Auckland.'

'Why that's further on from where I live! You could come with me for an hour, then go on to Bishop. You said you were going to walk. You'll get there just as soon if you come halfway on the bus with me.'

'I suppose so.' His voice was dubious. 'What about your mother? Won't she mind?'

She hesitated. Her mother would mind of course. It would be like taking some exotic species of animal home. But he would be made welcome as everyone was, even any stranger, in her mother's house.

'No, no, she would be pleased. There's always people coming in and out of our house. She's always saying she feels as though she's feeding the five thousand.'

It would be nice to meet a family, it was two years since he had been with a family. Holidays with a bachelor teacher, a simple Christmas with his father, just the two of them in a gloomy Southampton hotel peopled by ancient women with barking voices.

'All right, as you say, it takes me halfway to John Silkin's.'

She slipped half-a-crown across the table to him, mouthing that he should pay.

While he was paying the severe old woman, the bell suspended from the door trembled and rang and the two men in tweed suits, who had passed them at the cathedral, came in. They came across to where Roland and Lizza were sitting. Lizza stood up and took Roland's arm.

'Ee, why. Coom on, Jack, time we was on our way.'

The waitress looked startled at the change of accent, thrust sixpence into Roland's hand, glared at Lizza, and stalked over to sit the gentlemen at a nearby table. Mercifully she masked Roland from their view. Lizza nearly pulled him out of the room and on to the street.

'Close shave that!' Roland began to enjoy himself. 'Come on, where do we get the bus?'

'We need to go down by the river to get my case, I hid it behind a bush. Then we can go up through the town for the bus.'

They ran down the hill back to the bridge, causing a ripple among the people gathered in little groups here and there, enjoying their Saturday talk which was about more than the usual domestic and economic trivia of town talk. There were men on their hunkers against a wall near the bus station, and the notices outside the papershop declared concern regarding the imminence of a national strike.

14 *At home*

The click of the needles in the hands of the old women
followed Lizza and Roland down the hard-packed earth of
the back street. They sat on stools at their doors, knitting
or crocheting in the warm evening air. Sharp old eyes
followed their progress, an occasional voice called a greeting when its owner realised that Lizza Bremmer's body
lay under the fine green coat. Lizza called back in return.
She didn't stop to talk, but she never had, even when she
had lived in the street.

The gate and the back door to her house were open and
she shouted as she walked through.

'Ma! Johnnie! Bernard!' It echoed to no response from
within and then they were standing in the empty kitchen.
The fire crackled and heat radiated from the black kettle
on the hob. The table pushed back against the long settle
was set for tea, the sweet scent of home-made scones and
her mother's cherry cake encompassed in her the feeling of
home, and brought back the flood of feeling that rose in
her when the cherry cake had arrived in Bradford, in its
tin.

'Well, sit down.' She was quite sharp with Roland, and
pushed him on to a hard chair beside the fire. On the other
side was a rocking-chair – new to this house, though not a
new object. 'They've been getting a rocky-chair.' She sat
in it, feeling illogically annoyed. How could they get new
things, how could they change the house, while she was
away?

The gate slammed and Johnnie raced into the kitchen,
followed by his mother. They were both swinging milk-
cans.

'Why, Lizza! Old Ma Johnson told us you were here, but I wouldn'a believe her!'

He came and thumped Lizza, now risen to her feet, in a friendly fashion.

'Why, Johnnie! You must'a grown two inches!' She returned his friendly thump and turned to her mother, standing there as solid and certain as ever she had in Lizza's persistent dreams.

'Lizza! You came home! Is there anything wrong?' Lizza rocked on her feet to prevent movement towards her mother.

'No. Why should there be?'

The lie came too easily. As it came out of her mouth Lizza knew that she would never tell her mother, or anyone here, about her trouble. On the train she had imagined pouring it all out to her mother, and her mother folding her in her arms and declaring vengeance on the wrongdoers and that Lizza must never, never go away again.

She looked into the dark eyes, large-pupilled in the pale face, and knew that even if she did throw herself on her mother's mercy her mother would be embarrassed, and enraged in her own cold way, but would never ever hold her in her arms and insist that she should stay. She was innocent of the knowledge or experience that would help her to understand and sympathise with Lizza. Lizza decided at that moment that she had run her own life, kept her own counsel for the past three months. She would continue to do that, even here.

Her mother was looking at Roland who had leapt in a mannerly fashion to his feet, grabbing the soft cap from his head.

'Oh, this is Roland, Ma. He's – left – a school at Durham and is on his way to Bishop to see his – well, I thought we might give him a cup of tea.'

Mrs Bremmer put down her can of milk on the table and said, 'Well, he's welcome to a cup of tea.' Her tone suggested that anything more would be just out of the question. She looked hard at him, and spoke again, her tone much softened. 'You been in the wars, son?'

He put his hand to the gash on his head. 'No, I fell against a cupboard at school.'

The round vowels and soft tones sounded extra alien in this house, even to Lizza who had been listening to them all afternoon.

'You a toff, then?' Johnnie looked up with interest, having sat down to take off his outside boots.

'Shut up Johnnie! Don't be rude.'

He grinned up at Lizza. 'Catching a bit of it yourself?'

'Be quiet, Johnnie. I think that cut needs washing.' Mrs Bremmer marched Roland into the scullery, pleased to have something concrete to do. Lizza rubbed the top of her arms with her hands, and was treated to another thump from Johnnie.

'Quiet here without yer. Everything dead serious, Bernard with a face like a mile of bad road 'cos of the strike, and Bea and Renee moaning over lads.'

'Strike?'

'Yes. They've been locked out today and they reckon there'll be a strike from midnight on Monday.'

'The miners on strike?'

'Not just the miners. Railwaymen and transport workers, a General Strike. Kids who come a distance to school won't be able to get in. Not closing down though, worse luck.'

'Lizza!' Bernard, in clean Sunday clothes, was suddenly there. He put an arm round her. 'My, it's good to see you. You look bad. Is there anything up?'

Lizza glanced at the scullery door. 'Well, I've lost my job 'cos of our Ivy, so I came home to have a think. Been offered two more jobs so that's not the problem.' She sat down in the rocking-chair and he sat in the hard chair opposite. 'What's this about a strike, Bernard?'

'Don't you know? No, you wouldn't, head in the clouds or nose in a book. News of it must be round where you've been. General Strike from Monday night. The miners've been guaranteed support from the other Unions. This time we'll get some kind of right out of it.'

'Does that mean that there'll be no trains or buses?'

'There'll be nothing. Even cars'll have to get special permission to move around 'cos the pitmen are picketing all the main roads. I've got a meeting to go to tomorrow, in Chopwell, to fix up the organisation.'

Lizza's mind whirled on. No question of anyone following her if the roads were blocked.

'Picketing?' Her voice was careful.

'Yeah. Guarding roads and making sure that nobody goes anywhere without the say-so of the organising committee.'

'Does that mean I can't go back?'

'Why honey, there's no way you'll get back till after the strike, now, and if we have our way that'll not be till a fair and just settlement is made with the owners, or, better, till the mines is nationalised.' Bernard's voice was just a little singsong. He had obviously rehearsed these statements many times.

She felt a quick gush of pure happiness at the decisions being taken out of her hands. She had to stay now. Whatever Ma said or didn't say there was no way she could go back. The seriousness of the whole situation crept to the edges of her mind but at the centre was her own rejoicing at being home and having to stay there, safe from pursuits, safe from Ivy, from Gil, from Constable Mogdan, from Mr Mac's dead stare.

Ma brought Roland back into the kitchen, looking

considerably cleaner, with torn white strips of cloth
around his head. Lizza's mother's manner towards him
was soft and caring and Lizza wanted intensely the tender
touch that led him to the fireside chair. 'Move over
Bernard, this lad's not well at all.' She was right. The
cleaning had revealed a very pale and exhausted face, now
lying back against the wooden chairback.

Bernard's eyes lighted on Roland.

'Why, you're the lad off the bus, the one who . . .'

'Yes. We met that time in Durham when you were . . .'

Roland's eyes under the bandage rolled meaningfully
towards Bernard's mother.

'Yes, well, nice to see you again, marra . . .'

Bernard left the tired boy alone. There were other, more
important things on his mind than a runaway boy from
some prison of a school.

A quiet interlude with her mother pottering silently
about the tea-table, and with Bernard talking to Lizza
about Bradford and her working life, was interrupted by a
scream of laughter and pleasure as Renee and Bea came in
from work to find Lizza there. Renee hugged her and
hugged her and danced around while Bea smiled till her
face ached and murmured how nice it was.

Tea was a noisy and joyous affair, despite the doubting
and brooding presence of Mrs Bremmer. Roland, sitting
beside the fire with a cup of tea in his hand, watched with
fascination a family scene that was nowhere in his experience. The talk ebbed and flowed with a natural force
across beaches of trivial and serious thought. The food,
home-made and apparently plentiful, was relished, the
faces were full of energy and quick with life. He was tired
and the fire was warm, and he fell asleep with his head
resting awkwardly back on the hard chair.

Renee was recounting how disgusted her employer was
at this forthcoming strike, which would jeopardise de-

liveries to his grocery shops and impoverish his customers and himself.

'Called the strikers traitors to the kingdom.'

Bernard snorted menacingly. 'All right for him telling his staff about him getting poorer. It'll be a while before he'll starve. What about you, Renee, and you, Bea? You should be striking to show your support for the pitmen. Shouldn't be supporting the capitalists!'

'Capitalists?' Renee laughed. 'Aggressive dormice, more like. An' it's all right for you to say support, but you know that if me an' our Bea do that, there'll be no job for either of us to go back to anyway . . .'

Lizza sat amongst it, looking round at the faces of her brothers and sisters, not really listening to what they said, not really troubled at heart about the whys and where-fores of the strike. She was here. This was her family, this was her home, she had to stay.

After supper, with everything cleared away, the atten-tion of the whole family was turned to the sleeping Roland. Bea whispered, 'Don't tell us you're courting, Lizza.'

'Not like that at all.' Lizza was red. 'He just was in Durham when I was waiting for the bus and I was sorry for him.'

She went across and shook Roland's shoulder. He twitched, then sat bolt upright and stared around in amazement. He looked up at Lizza and his face split into a broad smile.

'I say. Forgot I was here. Thought I was still in school for a moment.'

'Time you was getting the bus. There's a bus to Bishop at five past eight, our Johnnie'll walk you down to get it. Have to go to the top end of the town.'

Roland stood up and smoothed down his jacket. Bea went to get the big travel coat from the peg in the back entrance. They were all looking at him expectantly, the only sound the ticking of the big clock on the mantelpiece.

'Well, thank you Lizza. Thank you all. It's never been so nice since I came from home.' He looked at Lizza. 'Perhaps I can write you a letter from Patagonia?' He was grinning, being her brother from the tea-shop. She nodded.

'Tell me everything you see.'

'I'll do that.' He shook hands with a slightly embarrassed Bernard. 'Good luck with your fight. If there is any justice you'll win.'

And he was gone, following Johnnie down the tussocky path by the houses.

Alice Bremmer was knitting when Lizza came back with her sisters, after waving Roland off at the back gate. She rested her knitting on her lap and looked across at Lizza. 'You'd be better keeping yourself to yourself, girl, not getting mixed up with strangers. You don't know what risks you're taking.'

All the happiness of the last few hours drained out of Lizza as though there was a tap in her foot. She gritted her teeth but the words came tumbling out.

'Why? It was all right for me to go away among strangers and fend for myself, as long as I was out of this house. You don't know who I've had to meet or what I've had to do in the last three months.'

Lizza spoke quietly, through gritted teeth. There was a shocked silence. Not in the memory of anyone there had any person of any age spoken to Mrs Bremmer like that. Lizza's mother picked up the needles and carefully trailed the wool in the proper way back over her hands.

'Go to bed, Lizza. And don't forget to say your prayers.' Her voice was hard, chipped rock. Lizza stood in some bewilderment. For three months she had decided for herself when to get up and when to go to bed – when she did anything. She looked around. They were all looking at her with concern on their faces, but behind each serious face she saw veiled and affectionate accusation. She, not their mother, had transgressed. It was not just her mother's rules that she had broken, it was the rules that reigned and gave structure in their everyday life. Renee broke the tension. 'I'm tired mesel', Lizza, I'll come up with you. You can do the fire, Johnnie.' She took Lizza's arm and moved her gently to the staircase, picked up a lamp in the scullery and led her upstairs. As the two girls undressed she looked affectionately at Lizza.

'You'll never learn, will you, Lizza?'

'What do you mean. It's not right, what she said.'

'Mebbe not, but it's her house and she can say it. She's mebbe a hard woman, Lizza, but she's had a hard life and has managed very well. Part of her managing has been knowing her word was law.'

'Do you never want to say anything?'

'Loads of times, but I just bite me tongue. I mostly do what I want though.'

'That's a kind of lying.'

'Mebbe so, but it keeps things nice and peaceful here.'

'So I cause trouble? Is that why she sent me away?'

'I don't think it's really like that, Lizza. Mebbe she sees that away from here you'll blossom, and staying here'd make you a one-sided bloom.'

Lizza snuggled into the edge of the bed nearest the wall, the least-favoured place that the youngest must take, with three in a bed.

Renee snuggled in beside her. Lizza's voice was muffled. 'Well, I think she was glad to get rid of me and doesn't want me back.'

Renee yawned. 'Really, Lizza, it's not like that. She mebbe hasn't worked it out exactly in her head, but her heart knows what she's doin', and she's doin' right.

You're different, Lizza, always have been. You'll go places, do things. She couldn't get you an education, mebbe she thinks this'll do instead. Hearth and home be our lives, and this is what she's training us for. You, you're different.' Her voice was fading, and she put her arm around Lizza, squeezed her hard, and fell asleep.

Lizza, pressed into the corner, cocooned in Renee's whole personality, felt more content than she had since she'd first left home. Renee's stumbling, intuitive explanation was much more acceptable than all the pattern of bitter reasoning she had gone through in the last three months. She went to sleep, warm and protected, very quickly.

She woke up two hours later, her face flat against the wall, sweaty and threshing about, her arm and leg in cramp, her back in agony. She clambered over the comatose lumps which were her two sisters, and stole the top blanket from the bed. The bedroom was cold and draughty. Silently she lifted the sneck to get out of the bedroom and crept downstairs. She wrapped herself in the blanket, got the cushion from the rocking-chair, and lay down on the thick hooked mat in front of the banked-up fire. She dropped off to sleep again very fast. The dead-faced image of Mr Mac had passed out of her mind.

15　*Nine days in May*

71, Fendale Street,
Brack Hill
County Durham
May 8th 1926

Dear Mrs Cobbett,

I am writing to you on this Saturday but I don't know when I'll be able to post it with the strike. They say nothing is moving on the roads and you can't get stamps. Anyway I did promise to write, and I'll post this the minute it's possible.

The strike is everything here. I arrived home on the day the owners shut the miners out. Then on Monday night the strike was declared so I was stuck here, whether or not I wanted to. My brother was annoyed that I knew so little about the strike. Said weren't they all talking about it at the mill. Well, I think they were but I was just getting on with my job and doing my thinking.

Anyway, it is all anyone here thinks about – nothing else. Bernard is in and out all the time, and some other man. Somebody has given him a bicycle and he is always off on it to meetings and things. The strike has made him cross my mother for the first time ever. One meeting was on Sunday in Chopwell which is a long ride away. It was an important meeting where they set up a kind of network of councils to run the strike and organise all the pickets. (You will know what pickets are. I didn't till Bernard told me). Anyway, the meeting meant no Chapel for Bernard on the Sunday morning.

Well, I had already told Ma I wasn't going and funnily enough she was quiet about that. Gloomy but quiet. Anyway, when Bernard said he wasn't either she went really mad. Talked about the strike being the devil's work. Anyway, give Bernard his due, he stood his ground. He was very red and very upset – though he's usually calm as a glacier. It took a great effort for him to withstand her, but he did. So the strike must mean absolutely everything to him, meaning, as he says, justice for the miners and all working men. So Sunday was very quiet with everyone walking on tip-toe just as if Ma would break like a china vase if there was the least sound.

I went for a walk in the afternoon with Bea and Renee. It was a fine day and as you walked through the town there was a strange silence (even though the people were around) just like the china silence in the house. But we were soon at the woods and the river. Renee is just like a little child when she's out like that, picking flowers, playing hide and seek, even rolling down grass banks. Bea is more sedate.

Well, on Monday midnight, as you will know, the strike was called. No bells seemed to ring. Tuesday was quiet as well as if a great breath was being held. Bernard took me to his allotment and showed me the rows of his planting, neat and soldierly, edged with late spring bulbs. I said it was very pretty, but Bernard said it could mean the difference between starving and eating in the next few months. He is getting so solemn now, and not interested in books or poems any more, though he did bring a pamphlet back from Chopwell on the works of a man called Karl Marx. I said I would read it but I haven't started yet. Maybe when I get back to Bradford I'll get the energy to start something new.

They all seem keen for me to come back to Bradford;

each one of them indicates that it will be best for me, and a large part of me agrees with them. But sometimes, Mrs C., I just die for one of them to beg me to stay, to give my support to the family. But it seems to me they are very self-supporting, and my skills are there to support me in throwing off the yoke and actually separating myself from them.

On Tuesday, Bernard had got hold of a strike bulletin, the first newspaper in these parts since the beginning of the strike. It was all about the justice of the strike and how the strike is an industrial not a political dispute, and how the strike was holding and more people were joining every minute. Did you see one?

Wednesday and Thursday were very quiet. The girls at work and Johnnie, reluctantly, at school. I wasn't allowed to do much in the house. My mother treats me as a guest and doesn't really say much. Bernard had heard some news on somebody's wireless. The Government are calling the strikers traitors and comparing them with the Germans, from the war. My mother was mad at that and came over on to the strikers' side. (Obviously the strike is not now the artefact of the devil!)

I hope you are well now, and your leg is much better. If you can find a minute to write I would like to hear from you. In any case I feel certain I will be back in Bradford soon. I'll have to find somewhere new to stay. Can you enquire near you to see if anybody has a room to let?

Well Mrs Cobbett, at least I'll seal the letter now and post it as soon as I can. I have needed to talk to you and the letter fed that need. I am often more a watcher here than someone who is part of the action.

Kindest regards from your friend,
Elizabeth Bremmer

On the Saturday of the strike week a motor-bike stirred up dust on the back street and screeched to a halt at the Bremmers' gate, and Bernard hopped on the back to go to a regional strike meeting at Gateshead. Lizza, with little to do as no one would allow her to do any housework, waved him off and wandered back into the kitchen. She sat at the sewing machine which was under the little window. If she opened the support flap she could make a working table for herself. The kitchen table was fully occupied with her mother's Saturday morning baking, done to make sure that there was as little as possible of sinful labour on Sunday.

She opened a narrow notebook which she had brought back from Bradford with her. In it she copied out phrases and ideas from books which she read, and now increasingly she wrote phrases and ideas of her own. She missed writing to Bernard, which had helped her get some ideas out of her head. Now the notebook was filling that gap.

She wrote for an hour but after that the day yawned very long. Her mother was carving the pastry edge of a plate pie, holding it up head high, reminding Lizza of some statue she had seen in an encyclopaedia. She put the notebook into her embroidered bag.

'I think I'll walk up to town and see our Bea at the shop, Ma.'

Mrs Bremmer looked across at her, almost surprised. They had been working together in a companionable silence. Lizza accepted the ritualistic activities of her mother which had been imprinted on her since she was born. Her mother tolerated the hunched figure writing at the flap of the sewing machine, the red hair glinting in the filtered window light. Speech was an intrusion. Speech was where their problems lay.

'Well, make sure you don't get under anybody's feet.' Her voice was inevitably sharp.

'I'll just be a minute or two, then up to see Renee. She'll mebbe spare a minute.' Her mother's head was covered by the iron door of the oven, and Lizza slipped out.

She hovered around the town for most of the day, first with Bea in the shop, then farther up where Renee worked. Renee found her a job to do – cleaning silver ornaments – while she was working, so they could work companionably together. Her 'family' were away for the day, and it was the housekeeper's afternoon out, so they had the run of the house.

The silver done, they wandered from room to room, fingering the clothes, reading the invitation cards, scanning the letters. Lizza wondered briefly if Dora did this at the Bamburghs'. She decided that she probably did. It was a certain way of gaining a kind of mastery over people who seemed to own you, body and soul.

It was early evening when Bernard came back from the Gateshead meeting. He had been there unofficially; for some bewildering reason the Miners' Union was still not officially represented there. He was angry at this but told Lizza that the strike was holding well.

'There's been no rioting, no need for soldiers. And there's no trams and no trains. There's no movement in the north except by permission of the Unions. Pickets on all the roads.'

'So it's going all right?'

'Long way to go yet. The big issue is the organisation and distribution of food. They'll mebbe use that to try and break the strike. But the regional committee has got it all organised.' His language was peppered with words reflected from the meeting. His eyes were shining and his face was proud.

On Sunday the house was brimming with people, men coming in and out of the house, interested in Bernard's account of the meeting. Bernard had them in the front room, the men coming in and out were in their Sunday clothes, smart and upright with a spring in their step. It seemed to Lizza, out on the margins, that the house was humming with fellowship and optimism. She wondered if it was a thing only men could feel, a community of which she could never be a member.

The thresh of people continued on Monday, the men weaving their way through the hanging clothes and washing apparatus as Mrs Bremmer grimly maintained her sacrosanct routines, even through the national crisis. Lizza sat at the sewing machine flap writing about world-shattering decisions made in the mist of steam and the smell of bleach.

National events were entirely eclipsed by the arrival of Ivy on Tuesday. There was supposed to be no movement on the roads but somehow she had negotiated a lift on the back of a motor-bike. The driver was a despatch rider going north with messages from one regional committee to the other. They were sitting at tea when she popped her head round the kitchen door, and Lizza's blood froze. Now they would all know about Mr Mac.

'Well, family! How's tricks?'

Her face was scrubbed clean of make-up, but her hair was bobbed and her dress was soft and fine.

Mrs Bremmer stood up. 'Well, Ivy. Sit down and I'll get you some tea.'

Lizza, looking around, realised that the smiles were all wary.

Ivy plopped down on to a chair and heaved a great bag on to her knee. Ma was clattering about in the pantry.

'What you got there, Ivy?' Johnnie got to the question she wanted them all to ask.

'Why, funny you should ask that, Johnnie, but I've got something here that might just be right for you.' She scrabbled in the bottom of her bag and produced a brown paper parcel which he ripped open with excitement that subsided when he saw that it was only a writing book with two pencils tied to it. She produced more parcels for the others. Strong, cheap scent for Bea and Renee, which they barely thanked her for. Bernard was more polite, thanking her with some charm for a rather elaborate silk scarf.

'Just what I needed, Ivy.' The irony was lost on her.

Ivy didn't read their reactions at all. She was getting excited, dancing and laughing. 'Ma, Ma,' she shouted, 'come in here and see what I brought yer!'

'Just put it down. I'll be in. Don't know why you want to waste your money,' the voice grumbled from the pantry.

'There you are, no gratitude!' Ivy giggled. 'Oldest daughter back from the wars and hides away, hides away.' Lizza wondered if she had been drinking as the giggling started again.

Bea suddenly spoke up. 'Stop being silly, Ivy, stop carrying on.'

'Stop carrying on, stop carrying on! Who are you to tell me to stop carrying on.'

'I'm somebody who can see you making a fool of yourself.' There were tears standing in her eyes at the effort to say something so severe to anyone.

Ivy got hold of her shoulder, clenching it hard, and put her face close to her sister's. There were tears in her eyes too.

'You don't tell me what to do, Miss Goody-Goody, Miss Please-Mother.' She started to stamp the floor with rage and Bea started to cry in earnest.

'You don't want me here – you don't want me here!' screamed Ivy. Lizza and Bernard stood horror-stricken. Johnnie looked on with a kind of clinical interest. Suddenly, Renee's square figure moved forward and she put her arms round them both, changing Ivy's stiff rage and Bea's rigid fear into softer, more sisterly shapes. She hugged and hugged them till Ivy's screams turned to whimpers and Bea's face returned to normal.

Lizza could hear the stubborn clatter of pots on the kitchen table, and Ma's brown paper parcel still lay on the table. She thought that for all her mad wailing, Ivy was right. Ma did want her away, and she wanted Lizza away too.

Dew still held the blades of tussocky grass spouting beside the worn footpath as Lizza made her way between the high boarded fences of the allotments. The May morning heat was lifting out the musty garden smell of pigs and hens and setting it trembling on the air as the creatures, grunting and squawking, came out of their crees for their boiled scraps and saved corn and chickweed. There was an unusual bustle and movement around the gardens. The miners, not working because of the strike, kept their foreshift habit, delighting in daylight and in growing things, always sustained in counterpoint to a working day spent underground. The strike, at least for them, meant building up a large credit of daylight to lay by against years in the dark, in the past, and they hoped, in the future.

Lizza lifted open the gate to Bernard's allotment, an old door on rope hinges. His plot was a large meandering shape at the edge of the gardens. Two-thirds of it was done over and well laid out with seedlings in orderly rows. The rest was a tangle of soft fruit bushes, high pushing weeds, heaps of decaying vegetable matter adorned with haloes of midges buzzing in the morning sun. At the far end were empty chicken-runs and pigeon crees and a small shed made of random bits of wood, sealed well against the draughts.

Inside the shed Bernard had his garden tools, a stool and a plank workbench. Lizza noted it when her brother had showed her round and had marked it as a place for her, away from the house. She propped the door open to let in the sunshine, flopped on to the stool and took a book out of the faithful embroidered bag and opened it in front of her. She pretended to read, staring hard at the print, but the words jumped in front of her. She wondered how long it would be before they would get to her, the people investigating Mr Mac's killing. The fright inside her about this was nearly as great as the sadness at losing Mr Mac. If Gil really had done it they would think she was in on it. Mr Mac. For the first time she let herself think about him in this quiet place with the distant random clatter of people going about their work in the gardens.

He had been her friend. She thought about the warm cluttered room, the cups of tea from china, the games with the poems and the words. She had taken all that without questioning at all. Then Ivy's sneering comments had spoiled it, had made her think of Mr Mac as maybe a different kind of man. It came to her that people had different kinds of selves, depending on whom they were with. Maybe with Ivy he was the kind of man she sneeringly hinted at. But with Lizza he was her dear friend, gentle and concerned, always there.

But he was not now. He was dead. Soon someone was going to come and blame her for it. She cried, without any sound, the tears coursing the stiff planes of her cheeks. She lifted the embroidered bag, put her elbows on to the dusty bench and leaned her face into the bag. She cried for Mr Mac, and cried for the stupid little girl who had sat in the warm room eating soup and reading poems, such a long time ago.

'Hey. Hey. What's this?' A hard hand had yanked at her shoulders. She lifted her face from the embroidered surface, tasting the salt on her lips. Ivy's face peered down at her.

'What's up with you?'

'Nothing.'

'Never known you cry for something, never mind nothing!'

Ivy leaned against the wooden doorpost, arms folded looking down at her, a little smile on her face, her dark eyes glittering.

'Well, little Miss Precious, you did leave a pile of trouble behind you, didn't you?'

Lizza had been waiting for it ever since Ivy had arrived. She had even thought Ivy would blurt it all out where her mother was, but realised that Ivy couldn't say anything without making herself look bad. Ivy had to wait for a time like this, away from the others. Lizza went into the attack.

'Was it Gil?' The course of her tears dried fast.

'Well, yes and no. Gil was there, when it happened you know, trying to get some reason out of the old boy.' She met Lizza's scornful look. 'All right mebbe he thought he might pick summat up. No good, Gil. I know that. He's like a bad habit that I keep trying to break. Well, anyway, they had this row and the old boy pops it there and then, wedged up against the door. Well, Gil's too scared to move in so he shoots out of the window.'

'Where's Gil now?'

'That slimy Mogdan came for him the next day, so now he's inside awaiting trial. For burglary, I think.'

She took a toffee out of her jacket pocket, carefully unwrapped it, and popped it into her mouth. Her cheek bulged.

'So, why d'you run off?'

'I was coming home anyway, and when I saw Mr Mac like that I just ran.'

'Funny that. Old slimy Mogdan asked a lot of questions

about you. Very suspicious he was. But I said that you'd planned to come away. Probably never saw what happened.'

She changed the toffee to the other side of her face, and brought herself eye to eye with Lizza. 'There. Ha'n't I been a right good sister to you? Looking after you like that? Gil wanted to put the blame on you, right square. But I stopped that.'

'I'll be able to go back?'

'Why yes. Old slimy'll want to talk to you, but you're all right. Second time he came round talked about a letter of old Mac's. Apparently the old boy left you a tin trunk with books in so he must a' thought summat of you. You'll need to see the constable though, when you're back.'

Lizza felt the vice inside her loosen and a lightness ripple through her body. She smiled at Ivy.

'Thanks, Ivy.'

'That's all right, our kid. Only come to let you know. Knew you'd be crinkled up over it. Took some doing that, coming back and facing this lot.' Her voice was sour and unhappy.

Lizza thought of the row the day before and sighed.

'What'll you do now, Ivy?'

'London, I think. Plenty of work there for a girl, even now.'

'What about Gil?'

'Well, I told you, I keep trying to break the habit.'

'Will you get a divorce?'

Ivy hooted a long laugh which had a very superior tone to it. 'No need. It was only a *kind* of marriage, our kid!'

Lizza's eyes were wide, her eyebrows into her hairline. Ivy reached out and clutched her round the shoulders.

'Eh, our kid. Innocence itself, but always knowing so much. Come on. It must be almost dinner-time, and I'm off straight after.'

They walked back through the gardens, arm-in-arm, Ivy's mind racing ahead to the fun and games which London promised, Lizza relieved of her guilt, skipping on light feet at last.

The afternoon light was fading as Lizza sat at the long table. The kitchen was uncharacteristically quiet. She moved across to poke the fire and it flared to contribute extra light. The back door crashed and the kitchen door opened and Bernard, white-faced and glittery-eyed, burst into the room.

'The bastards! The bastards! They've given up even when we were winning.' Lizza was rigid with shock. He might as well have invoked the devil in this house as use such language.

'Who, Bernie, who?' She took his elbow and pulled him into the fire circle.

'The T.U.C. They're supposed to be on our side. Capitalist lackeys, that's all they are. Cut our legs from under us.'

'Oh, Bernard, poor Bernard.'

She clung on, feeling helpless.

He pulled himself away from her and put his hands on her shoulders.

'No Lizza, not poor Bernard. Poor pitmen, poor workers, poor people.'

His hands came down, the door-sneck moved and his mother came in. She glanced from one to the other.

'They say the strike's over? That's just as well. The whole thing's too upsettin' . . . too upsettin' for us all.'

'Well, Ma, you'll be disturbed for a whole 'cos the miners are still out and they are staying out. Of course it does mean that things'll start moving, trains and traffic and things.'

Lizza's head turned back to Bernard. She smiled at

him, straight in his eyes. 'Well, that solves one of my problems. I'll be able to get back now.'

She could feel the easing of pressure on her right, where her mother stood. The decision was made.

Next morning Lizza woke early as usual. She was sleeping in the front room. On a made-up mattress, having endured a shake-down in the girls' bedroom after she had resorted to the fireside mat on that first night. Her mother had said nothing, just made up a mattress with new white cotton sheets in the front room, and told Bea that Lizza had better sleep there. Lizza felt again the ambivalent tremor of being a guest in her own house. The clock on the high dresser, its mirrors pearly in the morning gleam of the curtained room, showed ten minutes to five. She was about to snuggle back down and think about going back to Bradford, when she heard noises next door in the kitchen. Pulling a blanket round her she went through.

Bernard had the pitman's habit of early rising even when there was no mining to do. He was stirring the coal into life and tucking the kettle well over it on the hob. His nightshirt was tucked into a pair of old trousers and his hair was unbrushed, sticking out in all directions. He looked much younger than his twenty-two years. He smiled at her.

'You're an early bird. Hope I didn't wake you.'

'No. I was awake before I heard you.' She sat back in the new rocker, tucking her feet under her and arranging the blanket to fall round in a kind of skirt.

He went for another cup to put beside his on the table and measured out tea into the pot.

'I don't seem to have had the time to ask about the chair. Where d'this come from?'

'Same place as the allotment. The man was killed an' his wife took her kids back to Wales where her people are.

Needed the train fare so she sold the furniture for that. Didn't get much for it, not in these times.'

He lifted the bubbling kettle from the hob, poured the boiling water into the teapot on the table, very neatly and without splashing, and returned the kettle, adjusting it to an outside position.

'So, Lizza, you're definitely going back?'

'Yes. I think so . . . Bernard, I really *wanted* to come home. Wanted to come home like a great ache, thought everything would be right when I got back.'

'And it wasn't?'

'Well, it might have been right without me but when I was home it wasn't. Then when Ivy came I could see she had the same effect as me . . .'

Bernard protested.

'She does, Bernie. Mebbe for different reasons. She's not like me, I lived with her long enough to know that. But she's like me in that she's different from things here. And she's like me in coming home looking for something that's not being offered.'

'Lizza, if you think anything of Ma you've got to give a chance. You've got to try to understand her. Look at the way she's kept this family together since Da was killed, us going to school decent, seeing we're all well fed, helping other folks, performing her miracle of the loaves and the fishes when there appeared to be nothing. That takes enormous strength, Lizza.'

'Yes, but . . .'

'And being strong like that, having to be strong, forges you into a kind of iron, fine strong stuff, but unbending, rigid. So the people around her have got to mould to her or they get hurt.'

'But I can't change and be like our Bea, I can't. I'm like I am.'

'Yes Lizza, and Ma's like she is. Her strength, her fibre,

is in you more than any other. You were bound to come up against her. It's like her coming up against herself.'

'So she only cares about the ones who bend to her? That's a condition?'

'No, Lizza, no. All this is not about caring. It's about surviving together in four rooms day after day, week after week. You want everything put into words, into actions. She can't, even perversely won't, do that.'

'So she feels nothing for me.' It was like pressing on a sore.

Bernard gave her her cup of tea and sat beside her, squatting on the brass fender.

'You still don't understand. All this is not about caring, it's about survival as some kind of family. Everything must be sacrificed to that.'

'Me?'

'In a way, yes. She knows in her heart, if not her brain, that you are a kind of maker of change, that you could break up this family structure which is her, with your intelligence and need for liberty.'

'But change doesn't mean destruction, Bernard.'

'I know that. Look at the strike, look at it as it might have been. There would've been destruction. Destruction of a system that ground us down, made us less than men. But then in its place we would have built such a world, Lizza, such a world . . .'

There was enormous grief and loss in his voice and Lizza felt guilty. She put her arm round his shoulder as he squatted beside her.

'Oh, Bernie, I'm sorry, really I am. How can you stand it, me whining on like this when all that's happening. I'm really selfish, me.' She was stunned.

She realised all at once the way in which this strike had come upon her – vaguely there in the background of her more important experiences, only brought to the fore when she cynically wanted to display an interest in Bernie's happenings, to get him to concentrate on her.

Bernard smiled thinly at his young sister. 'Well, Lizza, there've been times when I could have shook you to make you look beyond your own head. Here is this world-shatterin' thing happening to the country and you're either on about Ma, or watching her with those clever unforgiving eyes of yours.'

He touched her hand where it came round his shoulder and his smile broadened. 'But then right from being young you've been on your own, playing about, making worlds in your head. Mebbe you can't change now . . . mebbe at this time what's going on in your head should matter more to you than the strike that's happening out here. Mebbe there'll be another time when you'll come and help us lot outside of that head of yours. Then you'll be a maker of change.'

Lizza released his shoulder and sat up straight.

'Well, anyway, I'm going. At least I know there's something I can do that'll please her.' She thought of something.

'Bernie, I've got some money that I've saved, that I wanted to give to Ma. But I don't know how, an' I don't think she'd take it. Could you keep it, then when's the need, use it.'

She went into the front room and came back with the embroidered bag. He looked down at the envelope with the pound notes in, and looked up at the stubborn face of his young sister. The gift both offended and amazed him. The whole of his being strained to return it. He looked again at Lizza's serious and tense face.

'Well. Yes, Lizza. Really useful, it'll be in the next few months. Could just make the difference here.' He stuffed it into his buttoned back trouser pocket. Lizza relaxed and felt quite happy. There was more than one way to be needed. Don't make a fuss about it. She picked up his change of subject.

'Do you think the pitmen'll stay out, then?'

'They stay out till the bosses is begging them to go back. Our so-called comrades may have deserted us, but we'll show them how to force just treatment out of bosses and government, we'll show them.'

The bangs and crashes above told them that the girls were up and Alice Bremmer appeared quietly through the stair curtain.

'You here in your nightie, Lizza? Not really decent now you're grown, and anyway you'll catch your death.' She had her day clothes on but her thick black hair was wispy and uncombed down her back. Just up from sleep, she had not put on the day's armour; Lizza felt her mother's gaze upon her. She stood up, gathering the blanket round her and smiled.

'Yes. I'll just go and get dressed. I've got a lot to do today.' Her mother's gaze cooled slightly and she nodded, then turned to Bernard.

'It's no work again today?'

'No, Ma, and not for a few days to come, I can tell you.'

16 Going back

By eight o'clock the whole family were sitting round the breakfast table. Just as they bowed their heads to say grace there was a loud knock on the front door. Lizza's head came up, startled, to meet her mother's gaze which was full of anguish and Bernard's which was full of amazement. Only two callers had ever used the front way. The back access was the total access to the houses in this street; there were not even paths up to the front doors, just a patch of green grass, then the road. Even the message from the War Office about Jo Bremmer had come the back way. The front door had been used by a tall, handsome, young army officer who had come to talk to Alice Bremmer about Jo, his brave death; and then by Mr Chilton, the cinema manager.

Bernard rose to go to the door. Mrs Bremmer put her hand out to stop her son. She slipped her arms out of her cotton apron, smoothed the sides of her hair, and went through. She opened the door and they could hear a man's voice mingling with that of their mother. Mrs Bremmer came through the door followed by a tall figure wearing a black helmet and a leather jacket.

'Somebody for you.'

Johnnie whooped. 'It's your toff, Liz.'

'Roland?' He looked taller, older, in the leather jacket, the scar had faded and his skin was pale against his white hair.

Bernard took charge. 'Ma, I bet the lad'd like a cup of tea.'

It was Renee who pushed the simmering kettle over the

hot coals, and took the warm teapot across from the breakfast table. They all sat down round the table, Johnnie making a space for the newcomer on the bench beside him. Roland looked across at Lizza, and her curiosity overcame her.

'Did you get to see the lawyer then? How did you come to be on a motor-bike? Aren't they sending you back to school?'

'Well there was a bit of chaos when I got to Silkin's, but he finally said I didn't have to go back. Said I could make my way to Portsmouth to see my father. His ship's docking within the week, now the strike's over.' He looked sympathetically across at Bernard. 'Sorry about that, Bernard.' Bernard's face was grim, quite old now.

'Not for us, it isn't lad. It isn't over for us. Anyway, how come you have a bike?'

'Well, I've been riding round on it during the strike, taking messages to the clients for Mr Silkin.'

'Scab,' said Johnnie, unemotionally.

'Shurrup,' said Bernard. 'Go on.'

'Anyway, nobody appears to have used it since the war because Mr Silkin's son was killed on the Somme. It was all greased up in a shed, wrapped up like a baby, when I found it. Well, old Silkin said I can have it, and I decided to ride down to Portsmouth on it.'

'It's a long way.' Bernard felt drawn to the boy, almost protective, the feeling he had had on the bus.

'I've got a week; and a tent and things.' He was untouched by any sense of difficulty. Bernard recognised the artless confidence, and was reminded of the sense of power and a sure future that emanated from his union leaders at the beginning of the strike. His heart ached.

Roland turned to Lizza. 'I thought I'd call to say thank you for rescuing me, and to give you the address of my father's shipping office in Portsmouth.' He pulled a paper from an inside pocket. 'You did say you would write to me.'

Lizza jumped up. She took the paper, but stared at him with mounting glee, a feeling of pure happiness.

'Not in a great rush, are you?'

'No, not really. Hoping it'll only take a couple of days to get down.'

'Why, then. You can take me to Bradford on your way down, stop over at Mrs Cobbett's, maybe.'

'Lizza!' said Bernard.

'On a motor-bike!' Renee wailed.

'On a motor-bike!' gloated Johnnie.

Roland smiled broadly. 'Well certainly! Why not? I'd like to.'

Johnnie pursued the implication and whistled reflectively.

'You mean to ride on a bike, Lizza? In them clothes?'

'Don't be daft, Johnnie, 'course not.' Lizza was grinning into Roland's face. Bernard was struck by how young they looked, like little children going on a Sunday School treat. They all turned to Alice Bremmer, like iron filings to a magnet.

Lizza's mother addressed Roland. 'She'd need to be really well wrapped up, she's never been strong, you know.'

The young man smiled down at her. 'She'll be all right with plenty of woollens, and I've a spare leather jacket and cap. She'll be all right, Mrs Bremmer.'

Johnnie, wide-eyed at this interchange, finally slipped out for a look at the motor-bike, pulled up on to the grass at the front.

Almost in a dream Lizza found her things and her mother helped her to pack. Mrs Bremmer brought out a brown knitted pixie hood with patterns round the edge, that had been Lizza's when she was at school.

'I can't wear that, Ma.'

'It's just the thing to keep the wind off your ears on that motor-bike. Here.' She turned Lizza to her and put the pixie hood on, tucking the side curls in just as Mrs Donahue had three months ago.

'There, that'n a few jumpers'll keep the wind out.' Lizza looked at the faint reflection of herself in the glass front of a picture on the bedroom wall, herself at eleven. She put her hands up to take it off, then said, 'Thanks, Ma. It'll just do,' and pulled on a jumper then a cardigan on top of that. Bernard laughed out loud and Roland smiled when she appeared but he reassured her. 'You're going to need it, believe me.'

By twenty-five past eight, Renee and Bea had raced off late to work, saying a merry farewell to Lizza that was very different from the last time. Roland and Lizza had to make their way through a crowd of children to get to the motor-bike. People watched from windows.

Bernard squeezed her shoulder. 'You take care of yourself, mind, and write, keep writing. I like to hear what's going on in that head of yours.'

She smiled at him from under her brown pixie hood, now covered with the leather cap.

'You, too. Let me know how things go, how this action turns out. They'll be asking me down there.'

He smiled and nodded. Despite the smile his pale face showed more sadness at the parting than Bea's or Renee's had done. Lizza turned to her mother, standing framed in the unfamiliar front doorway, her apron restored. Her mother looked in her eyes and smiled, a rare, brilliant, open smile, the smile that Jo knew.

'God bless you and go with you, child.'

Lizza smiled back and clutched Roland's belt as the motor-bike roared and threw up dust in the street as it rolled off. The whole street seemed to be waving to her from doors and windows.

She smiled into the hard leather back against which her face was pressed. Here she was, going off with flourish into a life which wasn't as strange or alien as the first time. She was going back to a known place, going back to dear Mrs Cobbett, to strange Iris and her fluttery mother. She was going back with a light heart on the back of a roaring black machine, behind a friend who was known, yet entirely unknown to her.

She felt confidence and a great sense of beginning.